SERMONS

TO THE

PEOPLE

SERMONS
TO THE
PEOPLE

ADVENT, CHRISTMAS,

NEW YEAR'S, EPIPHANY

AUGUSTINE OF HIPPO

TRANSLATED AND EDITED BY

WILLIAM GRIFFIN

IMAGE BOOKS | DOUBLEDAY

New York London Toronto Sydney Auckland

AN IMAGE BOOK
PUBLISHED BY DOUBLEDAY
a division of Random House, Inc.
1540 Broadway, New York, New York 10036

IMAGE, DOUBLEDAY and the portrayal of a deer
drinking from a stream are trademarks of Doubleday,
a division of Random House, Inc.

Book design by Pei Loi Koay

Library of Congress Cataloging-in-Publication Data

Augustine, Saint, Bishop of Hippo.
   [Sermons. English. Selections]
   Sermons to the people : Advent, Christmas, New
Year's, Epiphany; translated and edited by William Griffin.
      p.   cm.
   Includes bibliographical references.
   1. Church year sermons. I. Griffin, William, 1935– II. Title.
BR 65.A84 E5213
252'.014—dc21   2001058429

ISBN-13: 978-0-385-50311-2
ISBN-10: 0-385-50311-3

144915995

for

TIMOTHY JONES

on the occasion of his ordination

CONTENTS

Foreword xv

1 SERMO LI **3**

Advent

Birthday of Christ—Insoluble Problem or *In-
credible Day?* ⁘ *Bloody Games and Bloody
Martyrs* ⁘ *Ruination, Then Salvation,
Through a Woman* ⁘ *Fools Confound Philoso-
phers* ⁘ *Sour Notes and Hanging Veils* ⁘
Embarrassing Yet Encouraging ⁘ *Son of
Abraham, Son of David* ⁘ *Generations from
Abraham to Christ* ⁘ *Joseph's Justice, Sincere,
Not Severe* ⁘ *Doubts and Dreams* ⁘ *Handi-
ness of Heretics* ⁘ *Matthew's Generations—
Forty-Two or Forty-One?* ⁘ *Jechoniah Counted
Twice* ⁘ *Transmigrating and Prefiguring* ⁘
Jechoniah and Christ, Jews and Gentiles ⁘
Joseph, True Husband of Mary ⁘ *One Son,
Two Fathers* ⁘ *Mary, Model of Modesty and
Humility* ⁘ *Jesus, His Father's Son* ⁘
Christ, Son and Lord of David ⁘ *Marriage—*

Not When Limbs Are Locked, but When Hands Are Held ⁑ *Matrimonial Agreements and Arrangements* ⁑ *Two Supports, Nourishment and Marriage* ⁑ *Two Guides, Lust and Reason* ⁑ *Many Wives, Many Children* ⁑ *A Large Population in a Short Time* ⁑ *Maternity and Paternity* ⁑ *Two Fathers for Joseph* ⁑ *Adoption and Adultery* ⁑ *Sons and Fathers* ⁑ *Joseph's Genealogy, Not Mary's* ⁑ *Matthew Descending, Luke Ascending* ⁑ *Forty Generations in Matthew* ⁑ *Seventy-Seven Generations in Luke* ⁑ *The Number Seventy-Seven* ⁑ *At the End as at the Beginning—The Scriptures*

2 SERMO CLXXXIV **55**
   Christmas #1

Making Sense Out of the Incarnation ⁑ *Making Sense for All Present* ⁑ *Making Sense Out of Two Nativities*

3 SERMO CLXXXV **61**
   Christmas #2

Springing from the Earth ⁑ *Handing Down the Gift* ⁑ *If No Grace, Then No Hope*

4 SERMO CLXXXVI **66**
   Christmas #3

Who's Living Where? ⁑ *More Is Less, Less Is More* ⁑ *Picking a Birthday*

5 SERMO CLXXXVII **72**
   Christmas #4

Word Games ⁑ *There and Here* ⁑ *Changing and Unchanging* ⁑ *Extemporizing*

Contents

6 SERMO CLXXXVIII **80**

Christmas #5

Siring and Being Sired ... *For Whose Sake Was It?* ... *Obeying and Not Obeying* ... *Virginity Undamaged*

7 SERMO CLXXXIX **85**

Christmas #6

Night and Day ... *Truth Has Sprung from the Earth* ... *Comedown and Comeuppance* ... *Christ Generated Twice*

8 SERMO CXC **90**

Christmas #7

The Shortest Day ... *Two Nativities, a Novelty* ... *The Ass and the Infant* ... *The Time to Trumpet*

9 SERMO CXCI **97**

Christmas #8

Demotions and Demolitions ... *Passing Through Barriers* ... *Real and Symbolic* ... *Following Mary's Footsteps*

10 SERMO CXCII **103**

Christmas #9

Unusual but Not Unbelievable ... *A Cause of Joy to Virgins, Widows, Marrieds* ... *Truth from Earth, Justice from Heaven*

11 SERMO CXCIII **109**

Christmas #10

Congratulations All Round — Abuses and Excuses, Maladies and Remedies

12 SERMO CXCIV **114**

Christmas #11

Bodacious and Laudacious — Praise for Food — More Than Enough — Beginning of the Story   -

13 SERMO CXCV **121**

Christmas #12

Two Tall Tales — Birthing One, Birthing Many — Why Christ Came in the Flesh

14 SERMO CXCVI **125**

Christmas #13

Two Births — Three Chastities — Downsizing — Presbyters and Perpetrators

15 SERMO CXL **133**

Christmas #14

Faith in Christ — Compares and Contrasts — True God and Life Eternal — Only Christ Dared Say It — One Brick Short of a Load? — Belief Comes Before Understanding

Contents

16 SERMO CXCVII 143

New Year's #1

Against the Pagans ... *Clinging to Christ* ... *Building in Christ* ... *Hoping in Christ* ... *Speaking in Christ* ... *Arguing in Christ*

17 SERMO CXCVIII 151

New Year's #2

Greeting New Year's Day ... *Culling the Christians from the Gentiles* ... *Separating the Christians from the Pagans*

18 SERMO CXCIX 161

Epiphany #1

Christ Wastes No Time Joining Jews and Gentiles ... *Faithfulness and Faithlessness* ... *Shortcomings of Astrology*

19 SERMO CC 169

Epiphany #2

Epiphany and Manifestation ... *Herod's Terror* ... *The Blinded and the Sighted* ... *Gentiles and Jews, Co-Heirs*

20 SERMO CCI 176

Epiphany #3

The Tongue of Heaven ... *Gentiles East and West* ... *Jews, Custodians for the Gentiles*

21 SERMO CCII **182**

Epiphany #4

The Man Who Folded Himself ⸱⸱⸱ First Harvest ⸱⸱⸱ Jews Reveal Christ ⸱⸱⸱
The Latest Harvest

22 SERMO CCIII **188**

Epiphany #5

A World-Class Festival ⸱⸱⸱ Grace and Humility ⸱⸱⸱ Salvation of All the
Gentile Nations—Figuratively Looked At

23 SERMO CCIV **193**

Epiphany #6

Such a Great Mystery ⸱⸱⸱ So Near and Yet So Far ⸱⸱⸱ Walls Holy and Unholy

Appendix I **199**
"How Did Augustine Preach?" by F. Van der Meer

Appendix II **210**
"In the Midst of His Congregation" by Peter Brown

Appendix III **220**
"Never Without a Notarius" by Roy J. Deferrari

Bibliography **225**

Acknowledgments **228**

About the Translator **229**

FOREWORD

A.D. 391.
A.D. CCCXCI⁰.
Anno Domini trecentesimo
nonagesimo primo.

The Roman Empire about to burst; the Emperors about to cave. Theodosius I, kind of
wobbly in the east; Valentinian II, afraid of
his shadow in the west. Gathering energy in
the twilight, the Huns and Goths, the Van-
dals and Visigoths. Holding his own in
Rome, Pope Siricius the First, the thirty-
eighth on the throne of Peter, the thirty-
seventh to become a saint while on the
throne; thoughtful enough about sacerdotal
celibacy and ballsy enough to decree it. An
easy commute from Rome—three-to-five
days by ship in good weather—to Roman
North Africa. There, Numidia, a proud
province wealthy in agriculture, viticulture,
livestock. Its capital, Carthage, a flourishing
city with baths rivaling Caracalla's and
schools churning out *advocati* (lawyers). Not

far from Carthage, Hippo Regius, a port exporting thousands of tons of corn around the empire every year. And in Thagaste?

Well, in Thagaste it was springtime. A single rider at an easy gallop. Through forests of pine and orchards of olive. Across fields of wavering grain. Onto the grounds of a small run-down estate. Clattering in the courtyard. A mighty caparisoned horse uncomfortable on the cobbles. The Imperial Corps of Couriers, if you please. Message from Hippo Regius. *Urgent & Confidential* marked on the pouch. For Aurelius Augustinus's eyes only. Awaiting reply.

Time passed, the courier adjusted his seat, the horse dumped a load, and eventually Augustine wandered out. Well, the courier'd been expecting someone more sporting, like the anonymous writer of the famous graffito, lettered lacily across a wall somewhere in the environs of Thagaste. *"Hunting & Bathing, Laughing & Playing—That's the Life for Me!"* Just the sort of lad one could call upon in an emergency! Or so the courier thought. Instead he was greeted by a rather bewildered fellow, draped in gray drab, who seemed to be in another world.

And so Augustine was, and indeed living another life. Already he'd been there, done that, in Roman Africa and indeed in Rome herself. Yes, he'd succumbed to many of the charms of this life, but also he'd been awakened by all of the alarums of the next life. And here he was now, right where he wanted to be, a monk of the desert without having to leave the rather lush if neglected remains of his rather small family estate. An eremite in the grand tradition, and glad of it! Well, not exactly an eremite. He wasn't built to live alone. More of a cenobite, actually, what with some of the good friends he'd made over the last decade having joined him for a life of reading and writing, praying and studying the Scriptures.

The message from Hippo seemed serious enough. A cry for help. From a friend, also a member of the Courier Corps, who had immortal longings like himself. He'd written to say that the very salvation of his soul was at stake, and only Augustine could save him from the Ultimate Disaster! Would he, could he, come? *Cito! Statim! Quam celerrimum!* Date, time, and place were given for the rendezvous.

A trap—this was Augustine's first reaction—a classical example of imperial entrapment, but with something of a twist. The African episcopate had been in dodders for decades. To compensate, the concerned bishops in any number of dioceses, but only after prayerful collusion with their laity, began to sandbag, kidnap, impress into the episcopacy any halfway decent chap who happened down the road. That was why Augustine, since his return to Africa three years before, had been skirting the major cities and towns. For all his newfound humility, though, he still knew he was one of the few right enough for the miter and the crozier. As for his quondam hilarity, nothing'd stifle it more quickly than administration of, or admiration by, the masses, whether imperial or ecclesiastical. And then there was his perennial anxiety—well, that was why he expected a trap in the first place.

But his second reaction was, No, this wasn't a trap. It was just an act of charity for an old friend. And who knew, he might just quit the imperial service altogether and join the little community, the monkish band, whatever they were, in Thagaste. Augustine nodded, slapped the horse on the rump, and sent the courier off.

It was a longer trip than Augustine cared to make. Two hundred miles north to the Mediterranean, then east along the coast for some days to Hippo Regius, a roiling, stinking, thriving city. The trysting place was the cathedral, a church he knew well. He arrived early on the appointed morning, and enjoying the cool dark of the interior, shedding the fatigue of the journey, he began to recollect his soul.

That was when it happened!

A low rumble. The padding of soft feet on stone floor. The swarming of a crowd. Then singing, dancing, and what, chanting? All begging Valerius, Bishop of Hippo, who was just rounding a pillar and grinning like a cat, to make Augustine a priest right then and there. Yes, said the Venerable Old Geezer to the startled young man, it was a trap, but he had to make his move before another bishop snatched him up first.

Priest he became then, right on the spot, amid tears of confusion and disbelief. Punishment from God for the sins of his past life—that was the only way he could interpret this ghastly encounter! Priesthood was for dolts, big clumsy farm lads willing, for just a modest step up the social ladder, to shoulder the everyday burdens of the church; obviously not a happy step for an intellectually sophisticated person such as himself! But Valerius had this plan. He quickly made Augustine coadjutor bishop with right of succession to the See of Hippo.

For Valerius the mischievous deed had a palliative effect; he lived for another five years. Long enough for him to take great pleasure in watching his protégé swanning around, especially at the Plenary Council of Africa in 393, presided over by Aurelius, Bishop of Carthage, where Augustine distinguished himself by delivering, at the assembled bishops' request, a discourse on the articles of the Creed.

For Augustine, though, it meant bidding farewell to his bucolic surroundings and moving to the boisterous, business-oriented city. Valerius was helpful in this too, allowing him to relocate his ragtag community from Thagaste to Hippo, onto a rather nice spot in the cathedral garden.

For Augustine it meant also that he'd be doing something he was really good at. Valerius saw to that right away. A Greek himself, and a missionary bishop to boot in this *ultima Thule* of Roman madness, he never did get a handle on the roguish, vulgar Latin tongue; and he was hopeless in the Punic dialect at the outer reaches of his diocese. Hence, right from the start, he had his gifted successor preach in his stead. A remarkable faculty for the young man as it turned out, for at that time in the brief history of the Church, only bishops had the right to preach. Valerius knew that, but he just did it anyway, and the rest of the Church would have to catch up. And preach Augustine did, for the next thirty years.

Centuries later, it has come to mean that Augustine can preach to us. Hundreds of sermons of all subjects and all occasions. A fair number recorded even as he spoke. A few hundred surviving more or less intact. A seasonal sampling, the beginning of a cycle of sermons for the whole church year, is included in this volume.

Augustine's vibrant Latin has made for vibrant English. Reading these sermons today, we can still hear, in our mind's ear, his voice, loud and clear, urging and cheering, instructing and illuminating, fussing and fuming and sometimes even funning.

PRAISE FROM THE BIOGRAPHERS

How have Augustine's biographers remembered his sermons?

"Those who read today what Augustine wrote on divine topics do get something out of them," conceded Possidius, a fifth-century African bishop, longtime friend of Augustine's, his first biographer, and a saint in his own right. "But those who saw and heard him in person, speaking in his own church—ah, they were the ones who got heaven and earth" (*Vita S. Augustini*, 31). That was somewhere between 432 and 437.

"It is from the reading of these sermons," wrote Thomas Comerford Lawlor in the Introduction to his translation of Augustine's *Sermons for Christmas and Epiphany*, "that one obtains the best portrayal of the brilliant and profoundly spiritual Augustine presenting and interpreting the divine mysteries to the minds of his own people, of his great mind bending down, as it were, to nourish with the truths of God the 'little ones in the nest of faith' " (3). That was in 1952.

"Everyone who reads a number of his sermons will carry away the same impression as the men of his day," wrote F. Van Der Meer in his *Augustine the Bishop*, "for no words from the pulpit have ever so fully come from the heart or combined that quality with such brilliance as did the words spoken by this one man in this remote corner of Africa" (412). That was in 1961.

"In the unselfconscious routine of these sermons," wrote Peter Brown in his *Augustine of Hippo*, "we can come as close as is possible to the foundations of Augustine's qualities as a thinker. Seen in action at such close range, the cumulative impression is quite overwhelming" (254). That was in 1967.

So why haven't we heard more about the sermons? Lawlor's scholarly translation appeared in an academic series, published in 1952; it's long been out of print. Edmund Hill's translation of 89 sermons appears as a volume in a series intended to present all of Augustine's works in English; published in 1993, still in print, but aimed at, and priced for, the scholarly market.

Certainly, Augustine's *Sermons* have been overshadowed by *Confessions* and *City of God*, his two monumental works. And centuries of scholars have made their livings on his humongous theological and philosophical pile. In the few instances in which they approached his *Sermons*, and indeed his *Letters*, they've treated them as solemn highbrow productions. Which they really weren't. They were colloquial, lowbrow writings—mouthings, mostly—revealing the real Augustine, not the one we thought we knew.

THE VOICE

Latin was Augustine's second language, mastery of which bumped him up from the lower class in Thagaste to the upper class in Carthage.

Snobs in *Italia*, which Augustine visited once only but for a number of months, insisted that the squeaky African accent underlying his silken Latin rhetoric sounded through from time to time—the way a flat Aussie vowel would turn the head of a Yank or Brit today—but in Africa, where he spent most of his life, he sounded like, well, Cicero? Yes, Cicero!

As for the strength of his voice, there seems to be some question among the biographers. He himself had, or thought he had, a weak voice.

"May I please ask you to pipe down?" he once pleaded in a crowded church in Carthage. "After the strain I put on my voice yesterday, I may not last long today."

"Forgive me," he complained on another occasion. "You know how easily my voice gives out. So I'm going to begin with a bang, but I may have to end with a whisper."

"Yesterday!" he began on still another occasion. "Yesterday the church was packed, stuffed, standing room only. I tried to preach over the crowd noise. The crowd tried to speak over my noise. The result was that no one heard anyone else. So, if you want to hear me today, you'll just have to pipe down, and I'll do my best to pipe up."

The unpredictability of his voice on any given day depressed him, though, and the only thing that could rouse him from the depths was the thought that even the great Ambrose, whom he'd heard preach many times in Milan and had a voice like a bull, also got hoarse, and sometimes in the most embarrassing circumstances.

A final word. At least one person thought Augustine's voice sounded sweet. It was Eraclius, whom Augustine chose as his successor. Poor fellow, his inaugural sermon, preached in the presence of his celebrated predecessor, had some nice rhetorical qualities about it, but to the trained ear it was nothing but a rant about Augustine's voice being celestial and his own being abysmal. But he saved himself at the end with this particular comment. "When the swan stops singing, the cricket'll take up the chirp!"

THE AUDIENCE

Not all the sermons in this book were preached in Augustine's cathedral. But during his episcopate there probably wasn't a church in Roman Africa that hadn't heard him at least once. Nonetheless, a few generalizations can be made about his varying audience.

When Augustine preached, it was an event. Catholics came to hear him, the laity as well as the male and female monastic communities hard by the church. And when the spectacles and the gladiatorial shows were out of season, which was for most of the year, he also drew to his nave heretics and schismatics, atheists and agnostics.

Augustine was not only well educated and well versed but also well spoken, and his holy language was laced with all the linguistic entertainments that pagans thought were theirs alone. Indeed it might be said that, on any given holy day or holiday, he was the best show in town. Which is another way of saying, he entertained as he instructed, even as he carried on outrageous sidebars with the ever-present hecklers and jecklers.

As for interior church architecture in the region, there was no pulpit rising from the floor. Hence, Augustine didn't speak down to his audience. Rather, after the reading of the Gospel, the congregation remained standing. He sat back in his *cathedra* with the Scriptures open on a table in front of him or on his lap. The first row of standees was perhaps no farther away than five feet. They looked him in the eye, and he spoke directly to them.

THE SERMON

What did Augustine preach?

"The answer to that question," according to Van Der Meer, "is short and concise. His sermons all have their starting points either in passages in the liturgy, or in extracts chosen by himself from the Bible, and Augustine preached out of, with, and by means of, the Bible" (405).

"It was the Bible all the time," wrote Pope in his *Saint Augustine of Hippo.* "It is the quarry for all his doctrine; it is 'the word of God' that feeds his soul and out of which he 'provides old things and new' for the spiritual needs of his flock" (154).

"For Augustine and his hearers," according to Brown, "the Bible was literally the 'word' of God. It was regarded as a single communication, a single message in an intricate code, and not as an exceedingly heterogeneous collection of separate books. Above all, it was a communication that was intrinsically so far above the pitch of human minds that, to be made available to our senses at all, this 'Word' had to be communicated by means of an intricate game of 'signs' (very much as a modern therapist makes contact with the inner world of a child in terms of significant patterns emerging in play with sand, water and bricks)" (252–53). In other words, by means of words.

It was Augustine's habit to think during the day about the sermon he was going to preach the following day. Perhaps he even made it the subject of his meditation the night before. But when it came time for him to speak, with no notes, no prepared text, as was the custom of the time, he delivered it *ex tempore.* In the body of some sermons he even admitted that he'd tossed away his first thoughts in favor of an idea from the Gospel just read aloud to the congregation. Needless to say, because he always preached on materials that were dear to his heart, he was never at a loss for words.

While in mid-delivery he had no hesitation about sailing off in one direction or another. In the sermons that follow in this book, he worries about his parishioners, some who went to the games instead of coming to church, and others who, just for the fun of it, splashed about in the river where the pagan baptismal rights were taking place. He even wakes up those who've dozed off and, in at least one instance, he himself breaks off because it was his sermon that was the dozer!

HILARITAS AND SUAVITAS

According to his biographers, Augustine had, beside the usual orator's box of rhetorical fireworks, two, extraordinary virtues.

According to Brown, "the African[s], particularly, had a baroque love of subtlety. They had always loved playing with words; they excelled in writing elaborate acrostics. *Hilaritas*—a mixture of intellectual excitement and sheer aesthetic pleasure at a notable display of wit—was an emotion they greatly appreciated"(254).

According to Van Der Meer, "Clarity alone, if there are no other ingredients, can become as tiresome as a continual repetition of the same food, however nourishing, and so a certain charm, *suavitas*, is indispensable"(408).

THE COPYISTS

Augustine might not have written down his sermons beforehand, but they certainly were written down as he preached them in church. By whom? Roman society always had stenographers—Cicero had Tiro— and they were divided into three classes. Writing in shorthand from dictation or public speech, the *notarii* were employed by church dignitaries, and the *exceptores* by state magistrates. The *librarii*, often called *amanuenses*, transcribed the shorthand records into longhand. *Scribae* were copyists of longhand records only.

Hence, after Augustine finished a sermon, if anyone wanted a copy of it, the *notarius* handed the tablets to a *librarius* who'd copy it. The preacher then had the option of reviewing the copy, making revisions, etc. Once the copy was approved, the *librarius* handed it over to the *scriba* for further copies. Except in Augustine's case. Apparently, he delivered his sermon, then kissed it goodbye, never to look back at it again in any form. Fortunately for us all, copies were made, and copies of copies, and his sermons made the rounds in his own century and in every century since.

THE MECHANICS OF COPYING

Copying and recording in any century have never been easy; fifth-century Roman North Africa was no exception. The stenographer's tools were modest. The medium was wax, coating a rectangular wooden tablet *(tabula)*; keeping the surface of these tablets smoothly, freshly coated was an interminable task. The writing instrument of choice was the *stylus*; it could be made of wood, ivory, reed, or metal; no doubt every *notarius* had a clutch of each. As with writing instruments in virtually all media, *styli* eventually got smudgy, then sludgy; they required constant wiping and swiping if they weren't going to mess up. If the recording required more than one *tabula*, they were laced or strung together into a *codex*.

The *scriba*'s writing instrument was a *calamus*, reed or feather, whittled or shaved to a point. No doubt every *scriba* had at the ready a quiver of quills, fresh ones and spent ones awaiting resharpening. His medium was ink, jet black ink. Made of soot, resin, pitch, and fluid of octopus, requiring constant thinning, it was devilishly hard to get off one's fingers and, once on paper or papyrus, it had incredible staying power, much of it remaining legible to this day.

THE UNEVENNESS OF COPYING

Yes, we're indebted to the anonymous stenographers who surrounded Augustine whenever he spoke and took down his every word. To them and others like them over the centuries we owe much of the written culture of the West. And I myself, who've spent forty years in American publishing, writing and editing and doing all the other chores the *notarii* have done, would be proud to be counted among their humble, and indeed holy, number.

But, according to Lawlor, there was room for error.

"The copyists were often, unfortunately, quite lax in copying titles, dates, and places where the sermons had been delivered. Sometimes the texts themselves were changed in various ways. Thus in later years a single Augustinian sermon might exist in several versions, each presumed to be a different sermon. Again, in some collections spurious sermons found a place side by side with genuine ones. By the advent of the Middle Ages the contents of a new collection could depend on no more than a whim of the collector" (6).

That having been said, I doubt if many of us today continue to appreciate the difficult task of reducing the spoken word to the written word. Even with strolling stenotypists in the halls of Congress and miniature recording devices in the dens of the CIA and FBI, transcripts are notorious for their notarial errors. Hence, it's not so surprising to find in the text of Augustine's sermons many a sentence—indeed many a sequence of sentences—still needing adjustment.

THE DEFINITIVE TEXT

So, is there a definitive text of the *Sermons* today?

Well, no and yes.

Over the centuries we've been indebted to the scholars who've labored over the sermons to determine their authenticity and their textual integrity. Lawlor did the arithmetic in 1952. By then the number of authentic Augustinian sermons was 640, more or less, a number that since that time has been reduced to 138, give or take; and that's not including approximately 547 certified sermons or homilies explicating such scriptural topics as the Psalms and the Gospel and the First Epistle of St. John.

But even with that much ambiguity having been resolved, what's left of the text?

According to Van Der Meer, not a great deal.

"What is true of all good speakers is certainly true of Augustine, namely, that the bare text which has been reconstructed from the notes of stenographers does not even give an approximate idea of the reality. That stream of words that ceaselessly rushes on, sparkling and shimmering as it goes, has here been reduced to a shadow of its true self. One must have heard the man himself, writes Possidius, however well what he says looks on paper" (413).

Well, if the present text isn't *definitive,* may we say that at least it's been *stabilized?*

Yes, but the real question is, What's left? What's the residue?

Pure Augustine!

And for that we should be grateful. Indeed, we should rejoice!

Now the question is, how best to bring it into English?

TRANSLATION IN GENERAL

Sad to say, all translations are destined to fail, mine included.

"Translation will destroy the author's precise balance of thought, feeling, written word, sound," wrote Allan H. Gilbert in a brief treatment of the subject. "The loss is undeniable."

Currently, there appear to be at least three modes of translation from Latin to English that have any currency.

Parallel translation, or *transliteration*, is something of a misnomer. It seems to indicate two things.

First, for each Latin word in a Latin text there's a corresponding English word; denotation only; connotations need not apply.

Second, the word order, if it was good enough for the Latin, then it's good enough for the English. This is found in an *interlinear translation* of a classic work. As such, it's a handy device for learning a language while at the same time reading a classic work in that language. The New Testament, Jerome's Vulgate version, would be a good example.

Literal translation presents English that is fairly faithful to the original in at least two ways.

First, a hundred-word sentence, which isn't all that unusual in Latin, is rendered, out of fidelity to the original, into what will turn out to be a 200-word English sentence. That English hasn't been written in 200-word sentences for the last century didn't seem to bother the literal translators of the *Sermons* to date. The inevitable result is the canonization of the run-on sentence in English! Strings and strings of them! A terrible tangle! Rather like the orderly chaos of an academic procession gone wrong, what with the dignitaries being lined up, not in ascending or descending order, but according to the color of the robe or gown! Best rendered by academics. Much appreciated by academics. Not much appreciated by nonacademics (general readers).

Second, contemporary English abounds in contractions; but in vain does one look in literal translations from the Latin for an *isn't* or a *wasn't*, a *can't* or a *couldn't*. "Why then . . . *should not* the husband chastely receive what his wife had chastely brought forth?" (Lawlor, 51:26; page 57). Even the Latin contractions appear in an English without contractions; that's to say, in uncontracted form. The inevitable result is that Latinized English prose has an oddness about it, a candied, caramelized glaze surrounding the big red apple; not unattractive to the eye, but just try to sink a tooth into it!

Paraphrasal translation has a fidelity of its own, not, exclusively, as to the wording or word order of the Latin original, but, inclusively, as to its meaning. To that end, it does several things. It interprets the meaning of the original, appreciates the tropes and figures frolicking in the text, puts to work the connotations of words as well as their denotations, and tries to do them all into a readable, meaningful English. No more, no less. Best rendered by nonacademics who are writers (almost nonexistent). Much appreciated by nonacademics (almost legion). Not much appreciated by academics, who are nonwriters (almost by definition).

In summary, in all translation the loss of the author's precise balance of thought, feeling, written word, sound is, according to Gilbert, "undeniable; but it has been greatly exaggerated."

Yes, it can be done. And more easily by paraphrasal translation than the other modes of translation.

A saving word from Gilbert. "The merit of books lies in the beauty, richness, and adequacy of their symbols, rather than in the sound of their language. The greater the work, the less it will suffer from transplantation."

Suffering? How much suffering?

Well, it's been a truism of Latinists for some centuries that certain aspects of Latin style can't be reproduced in English—and that's what causes the pain. But I'd counter with a truism of my own. Maybe by academics they can't be reproduced, but perhaps, just perhaps, they can be reproduced, and rather easily too, by English writers of modest Latin pretension like myself. Without the suffering, real or imagined by Gilbert. And so I've done.

A final thought about *paraphrasal translation*. Despite its many virtues, only a few of which have been mentioned here, it does still appear, at least to academic eyes, zany, inane, bizarre, arbitrary, grotesque—and so it sometimes is—and hence the academics have concluded that it's false.

Yet, *literal translation* of a passage by two different translators aren't necessarily true just because they often appear identical; just as often they appear plagiaristic, the earlier by the later, which can't be true; the best explanation offered is that they err, yes, but at least in the direction of the one true literal translation.

But *paraphrasal translations* of the same passage by two different translators, or by one translator at two different times, can be wildly different and, contrary to the principle of contradiction, may both be quite correct.

"Every translation is inevitably an adaptation," wrote Gilbert, "substituting images that will give new readers the same idea and feelings the original work gave native readers. . . . The balance between the spirit and the letter shifts with every book, every translator, every reader."

That's why, he concludes, "an American with the soul of a poet and the training of a scholar may appreciate Dante in translation better than a Florentine cab driver in the original."

LITERAL TRANSLATION

At this point perhaps an example of literal translation would not be out of place.

Garry Wills ended his estimable Penguin Life of Augustine by quoting from a Christmas sermon (CLXXXVII, 2), intending it as an *encomium* to the bishop's immense literary and linguistic skills.

The words I am uttering penetrate your senses, so that every hearer holds them, yet withholds them from no other. Not held, the words could not inform. Withheld, no other could share them. Though my talk is, admittedly, broken up into words and syllables, yet you do not take in this portion or that, as when picking at your food. All of you hear all of it, though each takes all individually. I have no worry that, by giving all to one, the others are deprived. I hope, instead, that everyone will consume everything, so that, denying no other ear or mind, you take all to yourselves. Yet leave all to all others. Nor is this done temporally, by turns—my words first going to one, who must pass it on to another. But for individual failures of memory, everyone who came to hear what I say can take it all off, each on one's separate way (145).

May I say, the passage has never been better translated into English, especially with the severe, self-imposed restrictions placed on literal translators and translations to date. But, dare I ask it? Isn't this rather a rigid way of doing a foreign text into a modern language?

Hence, I've wondered if there wasn't a fair field of words beyond this, a fertile wordscape in which one could give a faithful and at the same time felicitous rendering that would produce something of the same effect the Latin original had on its first hearers.

PARAPHRASAL TRANSLATION

Perhaps, for comparison's sake, a paraphrasal translation of the same passage would be appropriate here.

Everyone here hears what I'm saying; that's to say, my words go in the one ear and out the other. But unless my words stop in your head long enough to be heard, they don't do you or me any good. Of course, if I whispered them into your ear, then only one person could hear them, and the rest of you couldn't. But that's not the point I'm trying to make.

Clearly this sermon as a whole has many parts; it's divided into words, and the longer words into syllables. But when I speak, all you hear is the sermon as a whole. Coincidentally but importantly, each one of you hears the whole thing. Which is another way of saying that you, whether as a group or an individual, can't choose not to hear some of the words, some of the syllables. A good sermon—if I may be permitted a comparison within a comparison—isn't like a good dinner where you can pick and choose. "The squash, yes, but not the squid!" In other words, you have to hear the whole thing, eat the whole thing, whether you like it or not.

And so it seems that the sermon text Wills chose can be rendered perhaps with equal faithfulness, perhaps even with additional meaningfulness, by paraphrasal than by literal translation. Indeed, the paraphrase seems to indicate that Wills might have been better off choosing another passage to praise Augustine to the skies instead of this one, which seems to get bogged down in the Ping-Pong of Epistemology.

And so, for this book at least, a collection of live Latin, recorded as it was delivered, paraphrasal translation would seem to be the best choice.

In his work *De rudibus catechizandis*, Augustine indicated that cheerfulness should be an ingredient in any agreeable discourse; that's to say, in any form of discourse that hoped to persuade (10:14). Supporting his contention, he cites Paul's Second to the Corinthians, that God loves a cheerful giver *"hilarem datorem"* (9:7). And so, I hope, a cheerful translator.

THE SERMONS THEMSELVES

These twenty-three sermons have it all, everything that has turned people onto—or indeed off of—Augustine in the past. Every compliment ever paid to him, every prejudice ever laid against him, may be found in some form or other in these few pieces of oral literature. They're also a congenial omnium-gatherum of information about his life and times.

Some random general observations.

About Christian humanism. The grand experiment of the monks in the Egyptian desert during the first centuries of the Christian era was a success in so many ways—Augustine certainly felt its lure—but in one rather noticeable way it was a failure. Its eschatological expectation that Christ was due back any minute now had died many simooms ago. Now Christians were thronging the marketplace, fueled by a humanism inspired by the Incarnation, and hawking their Christianity publicly, thus threatening every schismatic and heretic, every agnostic and atheist, they met.

About the new monasticism. New monastic communities sprang up, not only for consecrated men but also for consecrated women; and among the women, for consecrated virgins and consecrated widows. Among the latter was Augustine's sister, superior of a house of nuns in Hippo Regius; it was for her and her community that he wrote the letter that came to be known as the *Rule* of Saint Augustine.

About the anonymous woman. Also living in local religious community was the only really important woman in Augustine's life, his companion of fifteen years, the mother of his son. *Unam habebam* (I had only one woman) he wrote in his *Confessions* (4:2). In 1999 scholar Garry Wills did the gentlemanly thing. From the great drowse of history, he not only roused her but also, since nobody'd bothered to record her name, he christened her *Una*. It was with her, not with his mother—a high-maintenance matron if there ever was one—that Augustine passed through all the stages of true love defined by Plato, Cicero, Aelred of Rievaulx, Nicholas of Cusa, C. S. Lewis, the Greek and Hebrew Scriptures, and God knows how many others.

About the Jews. In Sermon 201, at least as recorded by Hill, Augustine's "attitude to the Jews . . . leaves rather a bad taste in the mouth; finding unfailing delight in contemplating their discomfiture, without giving a thought to texts he's constantly quoting himself in this context: Ephesians 2:2–22, and above all Romans 11. His attitude toward the Jews is distinctly less sour (though of course in no way ecumenically friendly) in Sermons 196 and 196A" (90).

About the shepherds. Augustine supposed the shepherds abiding in the fields were Jewish, but the shepherds in Israel today, mostly Palestinians, maintain that the biblical shepherds were Gentiles; that's to say, Palestinians.

About the solstice. "It adds nothing to the suitability of Christmas falling on or just after the winter solstice—in the northern hemisphere of course, and temperate climes. In the tropics and the southern hemisphere one has to think of other proprieties for Christmas falling in mid-summer, or the middle of the wet—or dry—season of the globe . . ." (Hill, 26). "In the tropics all days are practically the same length" (Hill, 49).

About male chauvinism. In Sermon 193 there's a reference "presumably to customary rituals and blessings connected with childbirth, and no doubt presided over by midwives. Augustine exhibits a characteristically male disdain, probably disguising suspicion and fear, of such feminine mysteries. . . . Male chauvinist to its very core" (Hill, 52).

Advent

Advent as a full-blown season in the liturgical year came to Christianity some decades after Augustine's death. That doesn't mean he paid no attention to adventual considerations as they now appear in the Scripture readings for the weeks, down from six to four, immediately preceding our Christmas. Hence, the first sermon in this collection (51). Was it delivered on a Sunday or a feast day? It doesn't appear so. More probably on a quiet day, or successive days, to what he hoped was a congregation of inquiring minds and searching hearts.

In it Augustine treats at some length such topics as the theater versus the church, the dueling genealogies of Matthew and Luke, the mind-boggling mysteries of Christ's two births, the gynecological aspects of the Virgin Birth, Joseph's shadowy presence in a number of venues, the several kinds of marriage, parenthood and parenting through the ages, strategies against adultery and lust, a little numerology, and, all throughout, the Scriptures: especially what to do when they're opaque, and what not to do when they're all too clear.

In a way this sermon brings the reader of the twenty-first century up to date with all the biblical issues surrounding the Incarnation at the time of Augustine. Whether or not they're debated as hotly today, it's still a pleasure to hear how the Bishop of Hippo instructs, and at the same time frolics with, his flock. Although not originally intended as a prelude to the festive sermons that follow, they're nonetheless the perfect preparation for them.

Christmas

The imperial Roman *Kalendarium* had its own feast days, with additions and deletions at the emperor's whim. Wanting to pin down a universally acceptable birthday for a venerable divinity, *Sol Invictus*, "the Unbeatable Sun," Aurelian (270–275) finally settled on the winter solstice as calibrated in the Julian calendar. As always, picking the same date, Christianity countered with the birthday of its own divinity, Jesus Christ, *Sol Iustitiae*, Sun of Justice. The date was December 25 around the empire; by early in the fourth century it was also the ecclesiastical date in Rome; by the middle of the fourth century, in Roman Africa.

Sermons 2–15 (140, 184–196) deal with such incarnational issues as the two births, one above and one below; the attendant midwifery; the concomitant emotions of pride and joy; the sonship of God and man; the sunship of justice; truth sprung out of the earth. Much paronomasia, horsing around with words; especially words relating to the Word, the words of the Word, the wordless Word in the manger, and all the other wordy and indeed worldly aspects of the Infant Jesus. Augustine's presentation of sexual fulfillment by angelic as well as animalic act leaves one gasping for breath. He compares the Word of God with the word of humankind. Pagan rites and practices are an omnipresent danger, but the Incarnation offers an aggressive hope. Arianism breaks out again, attempting to debunk the further divinizations of Jesus.

New Year's

Roman pagans had no trouble greeting the Kalends of the new year with mirth and merriment. But Roman Christians like Augustine had yet to develop a countercelebration; the feast of the Circumcision was at least a century away. In the meantime, in these sermons, 16 and 17 (197–198), Augustine had to dance as fast as he could, appearing as killjoy, then as lovejoy, trying to help his flock keep the faith. Once separate social communities, pagans and Christians were now inevitably bumping into each other in the *fora* and *balnea*—an incarnational humanism, as it were—learning to live with each other, liking to do business with each other, enjoying being married to each other.

Two observations by Hill, taken from his notes to the sermons.

"Ecclesiastical disapproval has, of course, never managed to suppress the rowdy celebration of New Year. For some details of what this entailed in those days, see Sermon 198. Perhaps . . . [Sermon 196] suggest[s] one kind of activity, mimic court cases such as are held—or used to be—on ships crossing the equator; or could there have been something like modern beauty contests, for the title of Miss and Mr. Hippo Regius?" (63).

". . . the circus . . . was the race track. The cruelty of the amphitheater had once, of course, included the throwing of criminals, especially Christians, to wild beasts and gladiatorial combats to the death. At the time Augustine was speaking, such things have been abolished by Christian emperors. The cruelty now consisted largely in the cruelty to animals now 'hunted' in the amphitheater by professional 'hunters' about whom he goes on to speak, and in the serious risks these hunters ran" (76).

Epiphany

"The feast of the Epiphany," according to Hill, "started in the Eastern Churches, as a celebration of the baptism of Christ quite as much as of the visit of the Magi. It was introduced into the African Church and other Latin-speaking Churches some time in the fourth century; and there the emphasis was almost exclusively on the Magi . . ." (81).

When the Magi stopped by to ask for directions, they expected some collusion from the Rabbis, but all they got was collision. The two groups of Learned Gentlemen had revelations of different sorts. The books of the Hebrew Testament on the one hand, and on the other the stars of the sky. Supernatural versus the natural. Odd thing, though. The Gentiles with the inferior revelation had the superior observance. And *vice versa*.

In Sermons 18–23 (199–204) Augustine got to vent a little about "stellar determinism" or "stellar dominance," a theory much in fashion with the pagan intellectuals. "What a flop that turned out to be!"

NUMBERING IN THE SERMONS

In each Latin sermon there are numbered paragraphs; for example, in the first sermon, there are thirty-five of them. But in this book these numbers don't need to be, and for reading purposes aren't, included. But if the need to refer to a paragraph number arises, please note that, for every number in the Latin, there's now a heading in the English.

BIBLE IN THE SERMONS

Augustine's Bible was sometimes the Latin Vulgate of St. Jerome, sometimes the many and scattered translations that preceded it. In this volume all of Augustine's citations have been freshly translated by me from the Latin of the Vulgate.

All references to the Bible are to verses as they appear in the Vulgate. Assumed is that these same references may also be found in the same place in the New Revised Standard Bible. Where they aren't identical in both Bibles, both references are given.

APPENDICES

As a serendipity, appearing as appendices, are brief excerpts from the major biographical works, detailing various aspects of Augustine's life as a preacher that have been generally known and available to the random scholar. To the random reader, however, even if they were known, they'd be unavailable.

"How Did Augustine Preach?" by F. Van Der Meer.

"In the Midst of His Congregation" by Peter Brown.

"Never Without a *Notarius*" by Roy J. Deferrari.

SERMONS

TO THE

PEOPLE

ADVENT, CHRISTMAS,

NEW YEAR'S, EPIPHANY

1

SERMO LI

Advent

BIRTHDAY OF CHRIST—INSOLUBLE
PROBLEM *OR* INCREDIBLE DAY?

How shall I address you, my dear Brothers
and Sisters in Christ? What's the appropriate
collective for a gathering of Christians? A
Quorum or *Quarum?* A *Choir* or *Quire?* How
about a *Caritas,* a *Sanctitas,* a *Felicitas Ecclesiae?* A Charity, a Sanctity, a Felicity Assembly? They have a nice ring, don't they?

It's December, my dear Charity in
Christ. As I reminded you the last time we
met, Christmas is fast approaching. And now
that Christ has aroused our seasonal expecta-
tions, He'll soon fulfill them all!

But before I begin, may I offer my usual
disclaimer. What I say here may appear to be
mine, what with my mouthing the words and

all, but as you know, nothing I say this morning is really mine. It's all
God's, I assure you.

The Apostle Paul said much the same thing in his Second to the
Corinthians (4:6–7). The Word of God is stashed in shapely earthen
vessels—that's us—but there's no mistaking a jar of clay for the Word
of God. And only when the pot is opened—need I say it?—does the
Word pour out.

But I've digressed. . . .

Last year, do you remember Christmas morning? You came to celebrate the solemn feast. I was sermonizing about the thorny problems
in the genealogies of Christ when a strange thing happened. I looked
up, and you'd all dozed off. Well, of course, I stopped instantly, promising I'd return to the sermon at some point in the future. And then another strange thing happened. You all woke up. Happily, we continued
the liturgy together.

That day I prayed God I wouldn't forget my promise. Apparently,
He's answered my humble petition. I've just remembered it, even if
you didn't, and I'm ready to make good on my promise.

As for today, there's no particular feast to commemorate, and I can
only hope that you're ready to hear me finish the sermon. I'll make
every effort to speak clearly—I promise you that. And you're going to
make every effort to stay awake—you should promise me that. Last
thing I want to do is speak to deaf hearts and dull souls.

A further word.

An ordinary day it may be on the church calendar, but it's also
right smack in the middle of the December gladiatorial schedule. It's
no wonder, then, that the church is only half full. The rest of you must
be in the amphitheater, looking more for entertainment than salvation.
I could say—*They've given themselves to games of the Flesh, as it were,
but have yet to pay attention due to games of the Truth!*—but I won't. Ah

well, for their salvation as much for ours, let's pray to God without distractions of any kind.

Now I know some of you dear folk won't join me in this prayer. I know for a fact that there are among you those who hate the gamers as much as the games themselves. Why? Because they're breaking down the good habits they've labored a lifetime to build up.

We human beings are funny that way. One moment we're up; the next moment we're down. Tears of joy when we're right; tears of sorrow when we're wrong. All that's very well, and such may be the cycle of life, but a certain steadiness of hand is required. After all, the Lord'd have us remember that the person who begins well doesn't always end up well. The Evangelist Matthew noted what He actually said. "The person who sticks it out to the end—sometimes to the bitter end—that's the person who'll be saved" (10:22).

BLOODY GAMES AND BLOODY MARTYRS

At best, the games are frivolous; at worst, frightening. Nonetheless, Christ has always wanted to shepherd back to His fold two groups of wandering sheep. The spectators who took great pleasure in them, and the gladiators themselves who made the games so riotous. Could the Lord Jesus Christ— *Son of God*, yes, but not unwilling to become the *Son of Man*—do anything more admirable, more magnificent than this, gathering those up in the amphitheater seats as well as those down on the arena floor?

And why not? Christ if anyone should know how it was doing battle with the lion and the tiger. He was once the spectacle Himself. How did that happen? Well, we have it on His own authority. That's to say, He predicted it. He pronounced it as if it were already fact. He had the eloquence of a Prophet, the elegance of the Psalmist. "They've pierced my hands and my feet. They've numbered all my bones. They've looked me up and looked me down as though I were a slab of meat" (VUL 21:17–18; NRSV 22:16–17).

He was ogled the way an amphitheater crowd with blood in their eyes ogled a champion in that wretched arena. He was spotted by those who thought Him fair game, but didn't have the common decency to root for His survival. As a matter of fact, they savaged Him with their voices and, as it were, turned their thumbs down. Yes, He made a spectacle of Himself by allowing us to make a spectacle of Him—I can still see them counting His bones.

And this was how He wanted the Martyrs who came after Him to be seen at the blood games. That was also how the Apostle Paul saw it and reported in his First to the Corinthians. "We've been made tiger bait to the world, and banquet fare for the Angels" (4:9).

When I used to go to these games myself, I noticed that people reacted in two quite different ways.

First, there was the sensualist response—people screaming and shouting as the Christian Martyrs fell to the jaws of the jungle cats, when their heads were cleft from their shoulders, when their carcasses were tossed into the furnace!

But that bloodthirsty response in other people, under some circumstances, could and did indeed change into a spiritual one. They came to watch the games, not through bloodshot eyes but, apparently, through angelic eyes. Oh they saw the bones broken, and they watched the blood flow, and they heard the heart-rending screams of the Martyrs. But then they came to see the unseen; that's to say, the faith of the Christians as they died the death on the arena sand. There was no sight at the games quite like this! A body being mauled while its soul remained unscratched. I know. I've been there.

Now when I say these things aloud in the church, you begin to see them with your own eyes; then, you hear them with your own ears. I know, many of you've never been to the amphitheater at all—you still loathe everything that takes place there—but my words have just now brought you right there, haven't they? I can tell by your tears.

And so may God be with you as you tell your friends who decided to go to the games today that they'd have been better off in church. Tell them about the games you attended with me this morning, if only in your imagination. May they come to regard them as vile, despicable, repulsive! And may they too come to consider themselves just as vile, despicable, repulsive for having derived so much pleasure from them.

Let us pray again. May they come back to church to worship God with us!

Odd thing, though, about some of those bloodthirsty gamers of the past. They came to love Christ because He couldn't be vanquished in the arena. There's no reason to blush about that. But it's a reason to pray with you, to worship Christ with you. Why? Because Christ only gave the appearance of being overcome at the games. What He was really doing down there was overcoming the world.

As we look back at it now, my dear Charity in Christ, He did indeed conquer the world. He made all the principates stand up and salute. He brought all the potentates low. Not with a proud banner but with a poor cross. Not by whanging away with metal against leather but by hanging like a lump from the wood. Suffering corporally, yes, but toiling away spiritually. Planted in the ground, the cross was raised high. His corpus wilting, He caused the world to draw itself up to its fullest height. Is there anything more precious, I ask you, than the diadem dangling from a crown? Well, yes. For the glowing, jewel-encrusted pendant, substitute the grimy cross of Christ. Love this God-Man, and you'll never be embarrassed in public again. . . .

I just can't seem to get off this subject. . . .

Bad it is when the spectators return from the amphitheater in a sad state; that's to say, when their favorites have lost! Worse it'd be if their favorites had won! Worst, they'd be thrice beaten; addicted to the amphitheater, enmeshed in Vain Joy, impaled on the trident of Cheap Greed!

However many of you, my dear Charity in Christ, had a moment's hesitation this morning before choosing the church over the amphitheater, one thing is sure. You overcame, not just another human being, but the Devil himself, the darkest, big game hunter in the whole world. But the ones who went to the amphitheater were overcome by that very same Devil; he could've been vanquished, though; others've done it. Christ Himself did it!

Overcoming the Devil, however, is possible only because Christ overcame him first. The Evangelist John recorded His words to His disciples at the Last Passover. "Yes, you can rejoice. I've conquered the world" (16:33). Yes, Christ is the Commander-in-Chief, the *Imperator Maximus*. Yes, He who had the temerity to submit Himself to temptation. Yes, the Devil tried his damnedest, not that he had much of a chance of succeeding against this Enemy. But why did Christ let this happen? He allowed it just to teach His military how to maneuver when under siege.

But I've digressed again. . . .

RUINATION, THEN SALVATION, THROUGH A WOMAN

Back to the point.

To become the son of a Human being, Our Lord Jesus Christ had to be born of a woman. But a question immediately arises. What if He wasn't born of the Virgin Mary? Would He have come out any the less?

Another question surely follows. What if He hadn't been born of a woman at all? Already God the Father had made a man without a woman; I'm speaking of the First Human Being, Adam.

Why a woman? Why not a woman? The one possibility is as good as the other.

Let's take a look at both of them.

If Christ didn't want to take up residence in a woman's womb, what would His reason be? Would He be contaminated by it? Or would His presence make that womb a cleaner, more comfortable place? I think the answer is obvious. Far from fearing that a temporary shelter was inappropriate for such as Himself, He'd want, I think, to show us a mystery of some significance.

Now as a matter of fact, dear Brothers and Sisters, I'm the first to admit it. If the Lord wanted to, He could've become a Human Being without renting a room in a womb, and all the Majesty of the Godhead wouldn't have paid Him the least mind. After all, He'd already made a Human Being from a woman without the assistance of a man. So why couldn't He make a Human Being without the cooperation of either a woman or a man?

I say all this because I don't want either sex, male or female, to despair of its own life-giving powers. And yet in the saying, I know that all the Mothers of the World will fret. Mindful of the First Sin, that the First Man was deceived by the First Woman, they'll think that they haven't a ghost of a chance of ever coming back into the good graces of Christ again. But I'd like to remind them of one thing. Christ was born of a mother and would be consoled by her femininity all the days of His life. That—even though He came into this world clad in full masculinity. There's a message here, and Christ addresses it to both sexes.

"Know, my dear Sexes, that to be a Creature of God isn't a bad thing. Badness came when Perverted Pleasure turned the Creature's face away from the Creator. It happened in the Beginning when I made the First Human Beings, a male one and a female one; that's to say, when I made a man and I made a woman.

"Now I'm not in the habit of condemning a creature I've just made.

Just look at me. I was born a man. Indeed I was born of a woman. No, I don't condemn the creatures; it's their sins I condemn. Why? Because I didn't make the sins; they did.

"Each sex should look to its own dignity, and each to its own iniquity, and in the end each will find its own hope. And as the Women of the World they'll surely find some surprises.

"When the First Woman urged the First Man to sip the Sweet Poison, is it so surprising that the damage was repaired through Another Woman?

"Is it so astonishing that this Other Woman made up for the sin of the First Man by giving birth to Christ?

"Is it so stunning that the Women of Jerusalem got wind of the resurrection of Christ before the Apostles did?

"Is it so unbelievable that the Woman in Paradise introduced her husband to the allure of spiritual death, but that it was the Women of Jerusalem who announced salvation to the fearful men who were huddled together in the Upper Room?

"Is it, finally, so dumbfounding that the Apostles announced the Resurrection of Christ to the rest of the World, but by the time they did, it was already old news, at least to the Women of Jerusalem and all those who'd already heard their good news?"

In conclusion, no one, neither male nor female, should feel the least bit upset by the fact that Christ was born of a woman. After all, how could the Liberator of us all be slimed by His contact with that lovely gender when, as a matter of fact, that gentle sex was already sublimed, as it were, by her contact with the Creator?

FOOLS CONFOUND PHILOSOPHERS

"It had to be easier for those who lived in the time of Christ; they could believe that He was born of a woman," the Heretical Hecklers could object, "but how about us? Who'd believe us if we make the same claim?"

"That's easy," I'd respond. "You can find it in the Gospel. Christ preached it. His disciples preached it. And I and others like me are preaching it today all around the known world."

But now the only sort of people who ask this question are the ones who are blind to the truth of the Gospel. They traipse around the universe raising every petty question they can. They even try to cloud the minds of those others who'd believe if they were given half a chance. At the same time they try to take up arms against what can reasonably be believed.

"Don't press us with the so-called authority of the world!" the Heretical Hecklers shout. "Don't use popular culture against us. It favors your position, yes, but only because you seduced the masses into thinking so."

"I seduced the populace into believing?" I ask in response. "This crowd you talk about, it was just a scattering of people."

"And we're not afraid of the Scriptures!"

"Nor am I. Yes, the Scriptures said the number of believers would grow, but when did it become a galloping multitude? It may've been visible to the Divine Eye, but not to the human one. And as for the so-called smattering who believed, there wasn't even that. It all began with just one man."

Let's take a closer look at him, this one man. Abraham was his name. In his time, at least according to Genesis, he was the only believer throughout the world, "among all the nations of the world" (22,18). That's to say, what this upstanding and indeed outstanding man believed then alone is now believed, by virtue of his progeny, by the multitude today. Then it wasn't seen, and yet it was believed. Now it seems, it's seen but is impugned. It was revealed to one man, and that one man believed it. Today it's believed by the masses, and yet a few still deny it. So much for the mathematics of belief!

He who fetched some fishermen to be His disciples and ended up including in His net every genus of authority—if this is to be believed by the masses, what more copious expression of that throughout the world can there be but the gathering, the *ecclesia,* the Church? Yes, the Church is the net, and floundering in its meshes may be found the rich and the poor, the noble and the not-so-noble, kings and their subjects, even the extravagantly educated and the excessively eloquent.

Yes, orators, scientists, philosophers, all were netted by those first fishermen, drawing them from the darkness of the sea to the lightness of Heaven. Let the Heretical Hecklers think of Him descending to cleanse by the example of His Humanity the great evil of the human soul, Pride. The Apostle Paul put it well in his First to the Corinthians (1:27). "God chose the weak things of this world to confound the strong things. He chose the fools to confound the philosophers; that's to say, not the true philosophers, only the pseudo-philosophers. He chose the things that are beneath contempt and that don't even exist in order to show us how empty they are."

SOUR NOTES AND HANGING VEILS

"Say what you want," the Heretical Hecklers trumpet, "but we know where to find the birth of Christ in the Gospels. And we get the meaning, catch the drift, of the Gospel words. Therefore, we know that the Gospels themselves disagree on the birth of Christ. If Matthew's genealogy's right, then Luke's wrong. Therefore, this disagreement disproves the faith. Therefore, before one can accept the faith, one has to show that there's concord, harmony, in the birth of Christ passages."

"My turn, my dear Heckle and Jeckle. Just how do you demonstrate this so-called discord, disharmony?"

"Well, for us it's a matter of reason and therefore an open and shut case," says Heckle.

"But for you it's a matter of faith, which is really rather sad," says Jeckle. "Faith has dulled your hearing so that you can't distinguish one sour note from another."

Well, so much for the Heretical Hecklers among us!

My question for you, my Dearly Beloved.

Could they possibly be right?

Let's look at how the Apostle Paul explained it to the Colossians.

"Yes, you've exchanged greetings with Christ Jesus as your Lord. Yes, there's no reason now why you shouldn't continue your walk with Him. And yes, He's the foundation, the structure, the superstructure of our faith" (2:6–7).

As the Colossians, so we too should keep the simple and certain faith in Him. We should even build an abode, a place where both may rest and refresh. That's the only way He'll open His Secret Self to us. The Apostle Paul again, from the same passage. "In Him are hidden all the treasuries of Wisdom and Knowledge" (2:3). He hides them, yes, but not because He's embarrassed by them; rather He wants to increase our desire to discover what's in these treasuries. A secret, yes, but isn't it tantalizing?

Honor Christ Jesus even though you don't see Him. It's as though there's a veil between Him and you. (The figure here is perhaps that of Moses who hid his face from his people by a veil; perhaps that of the Lord who hid His face from His people by the Veil in the Temple; perhaps even the scrims and screens of the well-to-do Roman who wants to know whom he's dealing with before he reveals his face.)

The more such divisions you discover, the greater is His honor and your belief. The more you honor these hangings, the sooner you'll both be face to face. Alas, there are those for whom these divisions make no sense at all. All I can say to them is that "the closer we move toward Christ, the more the scrims and screens are taken away"; or so the Apostle Paul wrote in his Second to the Corinthians (3:16).

EMBARRASSING YET ENCOURAGING

"Is Matthew really the author of the Gospel bearing his name?" ask Heckle and Jeckle, continuing their calumnious questioning.

"Yes," I reply with pious voice and devout heart, "Matthew wrote it."

"No doubt in your mind?" asks Heckle.

"No doubt whatsoever."

"Do you believe what he wrote?" asks Jeckle.

"Of course I believe what he wrote!"

So much for the supposedly pious murmurings of the Heretics.

As for you today, dear Brothers and Sisters, if you're secure in your belief, then there's no reason why you should be embarrassed about what you believe.

I was embarrassed once, and I blush to tell it to you now. It's about something I did as a young man. I decided to look into the Divine Scriptures, as every young intellectual should. I wasn't in search of piety; I just wanted to do then what the Heretics are trying to do now, damage their credibility.

Of course, I wasn't acting in my own best interest. My Lord had already come a-knocking at the door, but my life as a young man of the world slammed that door right in His face. What I should've been doing was knocking on the Lord's door. Instead I was only making things worse, slamming the door and nailing it tight. Proud puffin that I was, I was destined to fail. I dared seek what I now know could be found only by a humble person.

How much happier you are now, my dear Brothers and Sisters!

How secure you are, safe you are! Nestlings of the faith, accepting the Holy Morsels brought to you by the Holy Spirit!

When I was your age, I was a bum, a bogus. I thought I could fly, and so I left the nest. Of course, I fell to the ground! Not once, but many times. Each time my merciful Lord raised me up, a humble twittering *passer*, lest I be squished underfoot by a passerby, and put me back into the nest. Finally, of course, I did learn to fly. But I found this whole experience profoundly disturbing. I hope you'll find my retelling of it encouraging in the name of the Lord.

SON OF ABRAHAM, SON OF DAVID

If I may return to the crude interruption by the Heretics. . . .

"Matthew is an evangelist," they say, "but who'd believe a thing he wrote?"

"Well, I hesitate to say the obvious, but if we confess Matthew an evangelist, it follows, simply and quickly, that we believe what he wrote."

As for the genealogy of Christ, here's how Matthew put it down.

"The Book of the Generation of Jesus Christ, Son of David, son of Abraham" (1:1).

Son of David? Son of Abraham? How?

Well, it can't be shown except through the succession of the family. What I mean to say is, when the Lord was born of Mary, neither Abraham nor David was any longer in this life, on this earth.

"And yet, my dear Augustine," demand the Heretics, "you continue to say that Christ was Son of David, Son of Abraham?"

"Well," reply I, "why don't you put the same question to Matthew? 'Matthew, prove it. Prove that your family lineage of Christ was the true and correct one.' "

"Abraham sired Isaac," Matthew's text begins. "Isaac sired Jacob.

Jacob sired Judah and his brothers. With Thamar Judas sired Phares and Zaram. Phares sired Esron. Esron sired Aram. Aram sired Aminadab. Aminadab sired Naason. Naason sired Salmon. With Rehab Salmon sired Booz. With Ruth Booz sired Obed. Obed sired Jesse. Jesse sired David the King" (1:2–5).

Now, my beloved Brothers and Sisters, see how the lineage proceeds down from David to Christ, who, says Matthew, was Son of Abraham, Son of David.

"From the woman who'd been Uriah's wife David sired Solomon. Solomon sired Roboam. Roboam sired Abiam. Abiam sired Asa. Asa sired Josaphat. Josaphat sired Joram. Joram sired Oziah. Oziah sired Joatham. Joatham sired Achaz. Achaz sired Ezechiah. Ezechiah sired Manasses. Manasses sired Amon. Amon sired Josiah. Josiah sired Jechoniah and his brothers in the transmigration of Babylon.

"After the Babylonian transmigration Jechoniah sired Salathiel. Salathiel sired Zorobabel. Zorobabel sired Abiud. Abiud sired Eliachim. Eliachim sired Azor. Azor sired Sadoc. Sadoc sired Achim. Achim sired Eliud. Eliud sired Eleazar. Eleazar sired Mathan. Mathan sired Jacob. Jacob sired Joseph, the husband of Mary from whom Jesus who's called the Christ was born" (1:6–16).

So that's the lineage that proves that Christ was Son of David, Son of Abraham.

GENERATIONS FROM ABRAHAM TO CHRIST

Now that the generations as Matthew counted them have been faithfully narrated, the Heretical Hecklers raise their voices to push yet another calumny. It has to do with the sequence Matthew uses.

"Fourteen, fourteen, fourteen!" cries Heckle. "From Abraham

down to David; from David down to the Babylonian transmigration; from the Babylonian transmigration down to Christ" (1:17).

"So why," smiles Jeckle, "does Matthew add the following words? *So much for the generation of Christ who was born of the Virgin Mary.* What's she doing here? What place does a woman have in this all-male genealogy?"

Well, my dear Heretics, that's just how the lineage proceeded; that's how Christ was the Son of David and the Son of Abraham; that's how Christ was born and appeared among Humankind.

Note that this narration of Matthew's is the one we rely upon when we say we believe that Our Lord Jesus Christ was born of the sempiternal God; not only that but also that He's coeternal with Him who fathered Him before all time and all creation began. It's also the story of how Christ was born of the Holy Spirit from the Virgin Mary. Both of Matthew's stories are now our stories.

I know that there are others of you here today, my Donatist friends especially, but I'm speaking now to my Catholic Brothers and Sisters. You remember these stories—and indeed you already know this—to be an article of our faith. We profess and confess it today. Of those who came before us, thousands of Martyrs around the world have died for it.

JOSEPH'S JUSTICE, SINCERE, NOT SEVERE

What comes next will surely make the Hereticals howl out loud. Perhaps it's because they want to derogate the faith as it appears in the Gospel books. Perhaps it's that they think we've swallowed whole and entire everything Matthew wrote.

"His mother Mary was espoused to Joseph. Before they came together, she was discovered to be with child by the Holy Spirit. Her husband Joseph, however, was a truly just man. He didn't want to make a public thing of it, as he had every right to do; rather he felt it better to keep it a private matter" (1:18 ff.).

Now Joseph knew two things. He knew Mary's pregnancy was beginning to show. He knew also that he wasn't the one who put her in the family way. The only possible conclusion? She was an adulteress.

But "he was a just man," the Scripture says, "and he didn't want to make a fuss about it"; that's to say, go public with the story, a reading found in many codices; "he thought she'd be more comfortable in quieter surroundings."

As a married man, Joseph was profoundly saddened; but as a just man he didn't feel he should carry on about it. In fact, so great was his sense of Justice that he didn't want her to be branded as an adulteress; that's to say, to have her punished publicly, as was his right to do.

"He wanted her to be sent away without any fanfare"—that's how Matthew writes it. He not only didn't want to punish her himself; he didn't want to hand her over to others for punishment.

This is Justice at its most just.

One further thing to note.

Joseph didn't want to save the marriage just so that he could use Mary to satisfy his own lust. That's what a number of wronged husbands've chosen to do, take advantage of the lust lurking in their wives' loins. And just the opposite is also true. Offending wives'd gladly love their husbands senseless if it meant saving their own lives in the bargain.

No, Joseph was a just man and a loving man. He didn't want to keep her as a mistress; he wanted to enjoy her as a wife and a friend. No vengeance here; just a little mercy. Clearly, deservedly, he was the right kind of husband for her. She was with child—there was no mistaking that—but he knew she was also a virgin. How? Because she told him it was so. Yes, it troubled him greatly from time to time, but he, as she, came to see it as coming from Divine Authority.

DOUBTS AND DREAMS

The Evangelist Matthew continues.

"Once, when Joseph was bedeviled with doubts, an Angel of the Lord appeared to him in his dreams. 'No need to be afraid! Do accept Mary as your wife. As for the child in her womb, He was fathered by the Holy Spirit. Yes, she'll bear a son, and you'll name him *Jesus*.'

"Why *Jesus?*" Joseph asked in his dream.

"Because He'll save His people from their sins" (1:21 ff.).

You'll know, good people, that *Jesus* is the Hebrew word for our Latin word *Savior*.

To conclude this point, this we piously believe, this we firmly hold—*Christ was born of the Virgin Mary by the Holy Spirit.*

HANDINESS OF HERETICS

"Any questions from the Heretical Hecklers?"

"If I found a lie, just one lie, a misstatement, a misnomer," responds Heckle, "I'd have to disbelieve the whole thing, right?"

"Give me an example."

"Well," responded Jeckle, "I just have to number the generations."

That's how the Hecklers treat us. They begin by asking a question sweetly, then lead us down the flowery path to the Garden of Evil.

Odd thing, though. If we live piously, if we believe Christ, if we don't flop from the nest before we've learned to fly, then the Hecklers'll lead us—albeit unwittingly—to precisely where they don't want to go. That's to say, to the very mysteries they're trying to destroy.

What's all this mean?

Well, my beloved Sanctity Community, we Christians can't live with the Heretical Hecklers, but in a very real sense, we also can't live without them. I suppose that's just God's whimsical way of defining "handiness" or "usefulness." In other words, God sometimes draws good from bad people. As for their eternal reward, they'll receive one all right, but it'll be calculated from their own intentions, not from what the good God was able to drag out of their miserable efforts.

Judas is a particular case in point. As a direct result of his traitorous act, albeit in conjunction with the Passion of Our Lord, the nations of the world were saved. That's to say, if the Lord had to suffer, then Judas had to hand him over. God, therefore, liberates the nations with His Suffering Son, and at the same time punishes Judas for his shameful crime. Yes, mysteries lie hidden here. No doubt about it. But no one who has the least whiff of faith would get into an argument about them.

The conclusion is inevitable. The only reason we dig deeper into the meaning of the mysteries is that the Heretics, like the ones here today, heckle us and jeckle us to do it. In fact, once the Heretics get going with their rhetorical antics, they make little children cry. When the tots cry, they ask questions. When they ask questions, they beat their little heads against their mothers' breasts in a pathetic display, trying to make the milk flow the faster.

Yes, there's a ruckus and, yes, God responds to the ruckus. He enlightens everyone who wants to know, believer or unbeliever. But that's just how the Hecklers and Jecklers have proven themselves so invaluable to us. They're clowning around intellectually, trying to lead others into error, but at the same time they're clueing us into our own search for everlasting truth. The Apostle Paul put his finger on it in his First to the

Corinthians, "There just have to be heresies." Why? "How else would the truths rebutting them be broadcast around the world?" (11:19).

MATTHEW'S GENERATIONS—FORTY-TWO OR FORTY-ONE?

"Just look at the way Matthew counts when he lists the generations," the Heretics say. "Fourteen from Abraham to David. Fourteen from David to Babylon. Fourteen from Babylon to Christ. Three times fourteen—that makes forty-two. But when we count the generations, we come up with only forty-one. Is it any wonder, then, that we cry calumny, crack jokes, make unflattering comparisons?"

To that I'd respond, yes, Matthew does say he lists forty-two generations. But You count only forty-one. Well, so do I. How do we explain it? Well, it's a mystery, at least for us Catholic Christians. We rejoice in the good news of Matthew's Gospel, and we would've left it at that if you Hereticals hadn't kept peppering us. But no mind. The more you force us to dig, the greater the treasure we'll find. All of which is to say, my dear Heretics, stick with us. We're producing a spectacle that'll blow your minds!

Let's review the count once again.

Fourteen generations from Abraham to David. From Solomon, who's David's son, to Jechoniah, another fourteen. Then the transmigration to Babylon, which took place during Jechoniah's lifetime. Then the next set of fourteen begins with the same Jechoniah.

JECHONIAH COUNTED TWICE

Yes, my dear Sanctity assembly, there's a mystery here. I've already looked into it and found a satisfactory conclusion. And so I hope will you.

To make the third group come out at fourteen, Matthew used Jechoniah a second time. Why? Well, as you know, everything that took place among the people of Israel had some mystical significance. This was true of Jechoniah. He wasn't just a careless mistake on the part of Matthew.

If you'll pardon a homely example.

Suppose there were two fields and between them there was a wall or a fence. Whatever the boundary, the owner on one side measures his property right up to the boundary; and the owner on the other side measures his property beginning from the very same boundary. So as you can see, no need for Heckle and Jeckle, our beloved Hereticals, to get so huffy and puffy about it.

A plausible explanation, or is it? Why wasn't the common boundary principle used in the first two sets of fourteen? That's to say, the first set ended with David, but why didn't the second set begin with David? Ahhh the Great Mystery!

The transmigration to Babylon's the key, my dear Sanctity assembly. Jechoniah, upon the death of his father, succeeded to the throne. But through no fault of his own, moral or otherwise, he himself was bumped from the throne, and another ruler, far less virtuous, was put in his place. Then the great trudge to the land of the Gentiles began. Everyone, Jechoniah included, made the trip. The saintly as well as the not-so-saintly. Ezechiel the prophet. Daniel. The three young men who'd be tossed into the flames but not consumed. They all made the trudge as the venerable Jeremiah had prophesied they would.

TRANSMIGRATING AND PREFIGURING

There's some prefiguring going on here.

The Jews didn't want Our Lord Jesus Christ to reign as king, so they bumped Him off the throne even if they couldn't put a finger on exactly what it was that He'd done wrong. Not only Himself but also His followers. They all had to make the trudge to the Gentiles, as Jechoniah to the Babylonians. Jeremiah had foretold it, but there were other prophets who'd said that the people should resist the march to Babylon. Jeremiah was miffed. He called his peers in peering through the fog Pettifoggers! Pseudo-prophets! We who read the Scriptures are quite familiar with this scene. Those of you who've yet to read the scriptural account would do well to accept our version of it.

Jeremiah, using the words the Lord God prompted him to say, laid it on the line to those who didn't want to make the grand trudge. But to those who'd go He promised a measure of peace and quiet, cultivating new vineyards, planting new gardens, enjoying the abundance that'd surely come (27).

How does all this prefigurement work?

How did the people of Israel really pass into Babylon?

Where did the Apostles come from? Weren't they from the tribe, race, country of the Jews?

Where did Paul himself come from? "Yes, I'm an Israelite," he said in his to the Romans. "I come from the seed of Abraham, the tribe of Benjamin" (11:1).

Many Jews believed in the Lord. From them some were picked to be Apostles. According to Paul in his First to the Corinthians, more than five hundred saw the Lord after His Resurrection (15:6). From these, according to the Acts of the Apostles, 120 were in the house when the Holy Spirit arrived (1:15 and 2:1–4).

What does the Apostle in Acts say when the Jews spat out the Word of Truth? "We'd been sent to you first. But because you spat out the Word of God, we've turned to the Gentiles" (13:46).

That's how the transmigration into Babylon took place. At least according to the spiritual dispensation at the time of the Incarnation of the Lord.

But what does Jeremiah have to say to the transmigrants about these Babylonians? "If they're at peace, so you'll be too" (29:7).

And so it's not all that hard to conclude that when Israel was again passing to Babylon through Christ and the Apostles—that's to say, when the Gospel came to the Gentiles—what did the Apostle Paul say? How did he echo the words of Jeremiah in his First to Timothy?

"First of all, I implore that supplications, prayers, intercessions, and thanksgivings be made for the benefit of all Humankind; especially for their kings and constituted governments. Second, I pray that they may lead a quiet and tranquil life with all piety and chastity" (2:1–2).

Of course these kings weren't Christian yet, yet Jeremiah prayed for them.

Therefore, the voice of Israel praying in Babylon has been heard. The voices of the Church've been heard—they've become Christian. And so you can see that what was figuratively spoken of—"in their peace lies your peace"—has actually been fulfilled. That's to say, they accepted the peace of Christ and stopped persecuting Christians. Now in the stability that peace brings, churches are being built, peoples are planted in the fields of the Lord, and all the nations are bearing the fruit—Faith, Hope, and Charity—that's in Christ.

JECHONIAH AND CHRIST, JEWS AND GENTILES

To rehearse the argument up to this point.

Yes, the Babylonian transmigration took place during the lifetime of Jechoniah. He became king of the Jews, but the Jews didn't really want him as king. And so Israel made that fateful transit to the Gentiles. Figuratively speaking, the preachers of the Gospel made the same sort of transit from the Jews to the Gentiles. Why then, my dear

Heckle and Jeckle, are you so surprised, amazed, that Jechoniah was numbered twice?

If Jechoniah was carried in transit from the Jews to the Gentiles—pay attention now—then Christ went between the Jews and the Gentiles. But wasn't Christ Himself the cornerstone?

A note about cornerstones. They're always the end of one measurement and the beginning of another. So in a sense, the one and only cornerstone can actually be counted twice, albeit in two different and distinct measurements. And so it is that at one moment in history the cornerstone was Jechoniah; at another, Christ. That's to say, the one prefigured the other.

As Jechoniah wasn't permitted to rule over the Jews, off they went to Babylon. So Christ, as the Psalmist had predicted, "the stone the builders rejected, became the cornerstone Himself" (VUL 117:22; NRSV 118:22). That's how the Gospel arrived at the Gentiles. Therefore, whoever you are, wherever you are, don't hesitate to count the Cornerstone twice; and the number written by the Evangelist Matthew presents itself to you: fourteen and fourteen and fourteen. And yet there are only forty-one generations.

How does that work again?

When stones lie in a straight row, you count every single one of them, but when the stones go in a straight line for a short distance, then angle off in another direction, you count the angle stone twice. That would answer the question, how many stones are there in each direction?

So it seems to be with the orderly number of generations as long as it remained in the same people; but when the people changed, as with the Babylonian transmigration, Jechoniah became the angle stone or cornerstone. And by prefiguration he was counted twice: once as himself, once as a figure of Christ.

JOSEPH, TRUE HUSBAND OF MARY

Here's another example of intellectual clowning around from the Hereticals.

"Matthew counts the generations of Christ through Joseph's line, not through Mary's," says Heckle. "That can't be right. He wasn't the husband of Mary."

"Who says so?" I ask in return. "The Scripture says so, and an Angel says so."

"Don't be afraid," said the Dreamy Presence to the dreaming Joseph. "Welcome Mary as your wife with open arms. Yes, she's expecting a child. Yes, the child isn't your own offspring. Yes, the Holy Spirit's the ferret in the woodpile."

This will take a little explaining, my beloved Sanctity assembly.

Yes, Scripture is at great pains to show that the Holy Spirit was the culprit—I should say, the agent—here. But the very same Scripture is also at great pains to show that Joseph had parental and paternal authority over the Offspring. And He was ordered to do the husbandly thing; that's to say, give the Child a name.

Scripture also shows that the Virgin Mary herself was aware that the Baby in her womb wasn't the result of Joseph's embrace; yet she too calls Joseph the father of Christ.

ONE SON, TWO FATHERS

Notice how Mary does this. When the Lord Jesus Christ was in His twelfth year—that was on the terrestrial, not the celestial, clock—He spent rather more time in the Temple during the annual visit than His parents had intended. Why? Apparently, He liked to chew the rag with the rabbis; and they liked to test His knowledge of the Law.

While this was happening, His parents with their friends and relatives were on the journey home when, no Child! Out of their minds with fear, the parents rushed back to Jerusalem, and there they found Him in the Temple, pleasantly tussling with His elders.

What's so amazing to us who read this passage in Luke today is that the Word of God never stops chatting people up, and yet people aren't always willing to hear Him. But for Mary and Joseph it was a quite a different story.

"What have you done to us?" she asked. "Your father and I thought we'd lost you forever!"

"Well, the time had to come, didn't it, when I'd have to begin My Father's business?" (2:42–49).

Here Luke had Christ speaking in His Father's house, not in Joseph's house.

"But," rant Heckle and Jeckle, "Christ admits that Joseph isn't His father!"

"Patience, my dear Brothers and Sisters; patience! Scripture is long, but the time for this sermon is short."

Clearly Christ was reminding Joseph and Mary then, as Scripture is reminding us today, of two things. That He was truly the Son of God in Heaven. That here on earth Joseph and Mary, grieving tearfully at having lost their only son, were His parents.

MARY, MODEL OF MODESTY AND HUMILITY

At this point, my dear Brothers in Christ, we have to be careful not to overlook something of great importance to our Sisters in Christ; that's to say, how modestly the Virgin Mary behaved. She'd taken the Angel's word literally. She'd given birth to the Son of the Most High. She'd deferred to Joseph in conversation. She could've crowed about the honors bestowed on her, but she didn't. The humble Christ could've taught her humility but, apparently, she taught it to Him.

Mary had great reason to be proud, but she wasn't. The rest of womankind had less reason to be proud, but they still were.

We too could crow about her virginity, but the Evangelist Matthew didn't. He described her as a virgin but also as a nonvirgin; that's to say, a woman, an honorable state in Hebrew life. In Genesis, as you remember, the First Female was created from the side of the First Male. And the Author of Genesis referred to her as "a woman"; and that was before her virginity was taxed by the First Male (2:22).

JESUS, HIS FATHER'S SON

Yes, the Lord Jesus Christ did say it. "It's about time I got started in the Family Business." And yes, it does mean that God is His Father, but not in such a way as to deny that Joseph was His father. What can we possibly use to prove this assertion? Scripture can do it. The Gospel of Luke (2:49–51).

" 'Didn't you know that I had to busy Myself with My Father's business?' He asked them. Joseph and Mary, however, didn't have a clue as to what He meant. But the three of them did leave Jerusalem, and together they went down to Nazareth where He lived the life of a perfect Son."

Luke didn't say that Christ was subject to "His mother" or subject "to her"; He said that Christ was subject "to them." To whom? Wasn't it to His parents? Yes, to both His parents, His earthly parents, no further questions asked.

So much for the precepts aimed at women. Now to the ones aimed at children. They should do what their mothers say. Also they should respect their mothers' wishes. Why? Well, even though the world was subject to Christ, He also respected His parents' wishes.

CHRIST, SON AND LORD OF DAVID

So you see, then, my Brothers and Sisters, Christ did say He "had to be about His Father's business." But that didn't mean He was brushing His parents off. He didn't say, "You're not my real parents." It's just that they were His parents where the clock ticks; but God's the Father where there's no tick to the time. They were the parents of the Son of man; God, the Father of His Word and His Wisdom, the Father of His strength through which He shaped all things.

If all things were shaped or formed or created through that strength, that power, which according to the author of the Book of Wisdom, embraced all things firmly and disposed all things sweetly (8:1), then they were also formed, shaped, created by the Son of God. I'm speaking now of Joseph and Mary, the same people to whom He'd later be subject, albeit much later, as the Son of Man.

Again when the Apostle Paul called Him the son of David in his to the Romans, he put it this way. "He descended from the seed of David, according to the flesh" (1:3). But nevertheless the Lord Himself proposed a question to the Jews, which the Apostle Paul solved when he added the words "according to the flesh." That's to say, the Lord meant that He wasn't the son of David according to His divinity; He was really the Son of God, and hence the Lord of David.

In another place in the same letter, the Apostle Paul had some good things to say about the roots of the Jewish people. "Theirs are the patriarchs from whom, according to the flesh, comes Christ; He's over all, blessed by God forever" (9:5).

Again the words "according to the flesh"—He's the son of David, but He's also the Lord of David—"He's over all, blessed by God forever."

In Matthew's Gospel Jesus put this question to the Jews.

"Whose son is Christ?"

"David's," they replied, knowing full well that was what the Prophets preached. And of course He was indeed of the seed of David, but according to the flesh through the Virgin Mary who was espoused to Joseph.

"How is it then," asked Jesus, "that David in spirit called Him Lord when he said, 'The Lord said to My Lord, sit at My right hand until I put Your enemies under Your feet'?

"Remember," asked Jesus, "when David in spirit called Him Lord? 'The Lord said to My Lord, sit at My right hand until I put Your enemies under Your feet' (22:42–46). How could the Lord be His son?" The Jews couldn't come up with an answer. At least none that Matthew recorded.

So Christ didn't deny He was the son of David. That was because He didn't want the Jews not to know He was the Lord of David. All they knew about Christ was what happened on this earth; they had no idea what had taken place in Eternity. But how to teach them about His divinity? Christ put to them a question about His humanity. It was just another way of His saying, "You know Christ is David's son, but how is He David's Lord?" Christ didn't wait for the inevitable answer— "But He isn't David's Lord"—instead He continued His question, using David's own personal experience. "Your son," God speaks to him in a Psalm, "I'll set on your throne" (VUL 131:11; NRSV 132:11). Here together in one Scripture verse you have the son of David and the Lord of David. "The Lord said to My Lord, 'Sit yourself down right next to me'" (VUL 109:1; NRSV 110:1).

Is it any wonder, then, that David held his son as his lord? Don't

you have the same thought when you see Mary give birth to her Lord?
Yes, He's David's Lord because He's God. He's David's Lord because
He's Lord of all. He's David's son because He's the Son of Man. Same
Lord. Same Son.

Paul put it this way in his to the Philippians. He was David's Lord
because He had the form of God; because He didn't think it outrageous to be on a parity with the Lord. He was David's son when "He
dumped His divinity in favor of servility" (2:6–7).

MARRIAGE—NOT WHEN LIMBS ARE LOCKED,

BUT WHEN HANDS ARE HELD

There was this rumor that Joseph wasn't the father of Christ. Why?
Because he hadn't slept with His mother. Well, it wasn't true. After all,
it isn't the exchange of chastities that makes both a husband and a wife;
it's the exchange of charities between the two.

Don't doze off now, my Sanctity Christians! The argument is just
hotting up.

The Apostle of Christ in the Church would have something to say
about that in his First to the Corinthians. "All that remains to be said is
that husbands sometimes act as though they had no wives" (7:29).

To this very point, I know many of our brothers, albeit fruitful in
the faith, do the same thing. In the name of Christ, and with the consent of their spouses, they manage to contain the concupiscence of
their flesh without at the same time restraining the conjugal love they
have for their wives. If ever there were a conclusion to draw, it would
be something like this. *The less the lust, the more the love.*

After all, are the couples who live this way any the less husbands
and wives? Is intercourse freely given or legally extracted the only
characteristic of marriage?

As for the wives in situations like this, they're still subject to their husbands, as is appropriate for them; and in a sense the more they're subject, the chaster they become.

As for the husbands, they truly love their wives, as Paul noted in his First to the Thessalonians (4:4), "in holy honor" as equal sharers of grace; or "as Christ loved the Church," as Paul put it in his to the Ephesians (5:25).

Therefore, whether the marriage act is carried out or not, within the marriage or not, this is a couple, this is a union.

Would that all marriages were like this!

Would that just a few marriages were like this!

That having been said, there's no need to separate the couples who can live without marital intercourse from those who can't.

Just don't undervalue the intercourse of two hearts entwined.

MATRIMONIAL AGREEMENTS AND ARRANGEMENTS

Another thing to understand, my dear Brothers and Sisters, is how Scripture treated our fathers who married for the sole reason of having children with their wives. Some had many wives, but they invited them to their couches only to beget children, not to satisfy their lust. They were following the customs of their time and tribe; and for their sensitivity in this regard, we can say there was a certain chastity in their actions. For that we can honor them. But it was a whole other case when a husband wanted rather more than the marriage contract allowed; that's to say, he wanted more from his wife than procreation; that's to say, he violated that contract.

There's no mistake about what the marriage contract said. Its terms were recited in public within earshot of all the parties. One of those terms had to do with the begetting of children. That's why they were called matrimonial agreements. If it weren't for these, fathers would be handing out their daughters to satisfy the lust of strangers.

But parents didn't have to be embarrassed when they gave their daughters in marriage. The fathers became in-laws, not pimps or panders or procurers. On hearing the venerable words about begetting children, the father's expression brightened, lightened up. As for the husband-to-be, what happened to his expression? Well, if he took her for any other reason than children, he should've turned red as a beet.

Let me say something I've said before. If husband or wife can't fulfill this term of the matrimonial agreement, then let them go to the debtors and collect the debt. And let them console themselves in their own infirmity. Please note, the husband shouldn't go to another woman; nor the wife, to another man. That'd be adultery. By the way, that's also the source of the word "adultery," to go "to another." But if the husband and wife should go beyond the terms of the matrimonial pact just for the lust of it, then they should do it in their own bed and no other.

A question arises.

Isn't it a sin to exact the marital debt—that's to say, have intercourse—more often than the procreation of children allows? Well, yes, it's a sin, but a venial one. My authority for saying this is the Apostle Paul in his First to the Corinthians: "I say this with compassion, not with command, in my voice" (7:6).

Another observation in this regard, again from the same source.

"You couples shouldn't defraud each other. That's to say, you shouldn't violate the marital debt you owe to each other. Unless of course you both agree to do so, and then only for a time, which time you should spend in prayer; then you should return to each other. Why? Lest Satan stifle your self-control." Again from First Corinthians (7:5).

What did Paul mean here? You shouldn't impose on yourselves too rigorous a requirement. That's to say, too much continence could force a spouse to consider adultery as an alternative.

Please note again Paul's distinction here. Was He ordering such behavior or merely allowing it? The latter really. In other words, that was how he regulated his own behavior; but he knew others mightn't be able to do the same. In other words, it was his way of saying, "I'm not ordering you to do it this way, but I forgive you if you do."

TWO SUPPORTS, NOURISHMENT AND MARRIAGE

My Brothers and Sisters, here's another point for your attention. Many great men did indeed have wives for the purpose of procreation, and we have the documentation to prove it. But what I want to consider now is, if they could have children without having to bed their wives, would they consider it a kindness, a privilege, a joy? Yes, I think they would.

Please note, there are two carnal activities upon which the survival of the Human Race depends. The prudent and the holy descend to them as a matter of duty. The not-so-prudent and the holier-than-thou fall head-over-heels into them. On the one hand it's duty; on the other, lust.

Now what are these two things?

First, eating and drinking. They're necessary, sometimes even pleasant, activities. If you don't eat and drink, you'll die. Nature tells us this. It's the one prop that sustains all life.

Second, marrying. It's necessary for the human race to survive. We each have our own lives to live, but eventually we die. But if we want the human race to continue, we have to marry and procreate children. As Jesus son of Sirach put it (Ecclesiasticus 14:18–19), the human race is like the foliage on a tree; as with an olive or a laurel, there are always some leaves, but not necessarily the same leaves. The trees are always dressing and undressing, but they're never unclothed. People die every day, and we hardly notice it. Why? Because on the very same day people are born, and so the human race survives. If no human beings came into the world, if no leaves grew on the trees, the earth would soon lose its life.

TWO GUIDES, LUST AND REASON

Yes, the human race depends on two things, but enough has been said about that. To each the wise, prudent, faithful person descends out of a certain sense of duty or obligation. He or she doesn't throw all caution to the wind and rush headlong into them. But how many eat and drink as though there were no tomorrow! Instead of nibbling and sipping, they gorge and binge!

Every book of Wisdom, spiritual as well as natural, but especially Divine Scripture, reprimands gluttons and drunkards. Poor souls, their God, according to Paul in his to the Philippians, is their gullet (3:19).

Some need no more than a whiff to bring them back to the table, even though they'd left it only moments before. And with no ceremony whatsoever, again they fall upon their food and drink like animals.

Others have a certain daintiness about them. They deign to come to table only when their appetite requires them. That's to say, they eat and drink to live, not the other way around.

If these prudent and temperate people were offered the opportunity of living without the help of food and drink, they'd count it a kindness and accept it gladly. No more condescending for them. No danger any longer of their collapsing into epicurean ruin. The Lord'd always sustain them in a pinch.

How do you think the saintly Elias acted when he received a jar of water and a hotcake every day for forty days (VUL 3 Kings, 19:6–8; NRSV 1 Kings 19:6–8)? With great joy, that's how, for he ate and drank out of duty, not out of slavery to food and drink.

Try to imagine this same restraint on the person who's placed his whole beatitude and felicity on the banquet table! He'd be like cattle in a barn. He'd hate your kindness; he'd be repelled by it; he'd think it a pain.

The same is true in that other duty, the marital one. One sort of husband searches for a wife among women he thinks will satisfy his lust. But that sort of woman is hardly ever the satisfying kind. If men like him can't or won't get rid of their lust, I'd suggest they try to keep it within the confines of the marital bed and the marital bond. And that's about as much as I'll concede to human infirmity.

Odd thing, though.

Ask a man like that a plain question. "Why do you marry a woman at all?" He'd probably have a sheepish answer. "To have children." But if someone else spoke to him, someone he trusted, and said, "God's powerful enough to give you, and indeed He will give you, children even without your doing the marital deed with your wife." Then and there he'd have to confess that it wasn't just children he wanted when he went a-wiving. Let's hope he confesses his weakness and welcomes the children he was pretending to receive out of duty.

MANY WIVES, MANY CHILDREN

So those holy godly men of yore, the Patriarchs, my dear Men and Women of God, sought children; yes, they wanted to raise children. To achieve that goal they were joined to women; for this purpose they had intercourse with women to procreate children. And so it was permitted to them to have a number of wives. If unbridled lust were a virtue pleasing to God at that moment in history, He would've permitted one woman to have many husbands; that'd give her parity with the man who could have many wives.

Why didn't all the chaste women have more than one husband? Could it be that many women had one husband because it had something to do with the numerosity of the race? If that's the norm, then one woman with many men couldn't increase the productivity of the race the way one man with many women can.

Wherefore, my dear Brothers and Sisters, if our Patriarchs married women and serviced them for no other reason than siring children, then they would've been more than pleased, wouldn't they? if they could've had the children without the intercourse. What I mean to say is, they did what they did, not for the lust of it, but for the duty.

All of which brings us back to Joseph. Wasn't he still a father even if he got his son through a route other than concupiscence? Far be it that Christian chastity should have something to do with it! Certainly Jewish chastity had nothing to do with it at all!

To conclude this point, love your wives, but love them chastely. Do the animal thing but only for the begetting of children. Because it's the only way to do it, then do it, but wistfully, wishing there were a better way. Count it as a residue of our common father, Adam.

Now there's no need to trumpet his punishment. He brought it upon himself when he sinned; and from that moment on his children were mortal. Unfortunately, this punishment is still in place; God hasn't taken it away; He's left it behind as a token of where Humankind has been and where it's headed. It's also a token of His embrace—an embrace that hasn't a whiff of corruption, a sniff of punishment about it.

A LARGE POPULATION IN A SHORT TIME

There was a reason for all this. That nation, Israel, from its beginnings down to the time of Christ, had to acquire a large population in a short period of time. Why? There'd been a lot of prefiguring going on in the Scriptures, especially with regard to the Church, and it took a lot of population to carry it off. Hence, the custom of one man taking an assortment of wives helped achieve that national goal.

MATERNITY AND PATERNITY

Before the King of all the nations Himself was born, a woman's virginity had no value among the Jews. Maternity—that was a woman's highest honor. That is, until Mary the Mother of Our Lord came along. She gave birth to a son and didn't lose her virginity in the process. Hers was a legal marriage, a marriage without intercourse, but not without hugs and kisses.

And so I put this question to you. It's about Mary's chastity.

Why can't her husband receive chastely the baby she brought into this world chastely?

Another question.

If she was chaste as a wife and he as a husband, why can't they both be chaste as mother and father?

What are the Hecklers and Jecklers shouting now?

"Joseph shouldn't be called father because he didn't do the siring himself!"

Well, that's just the sort of crack that says it's the lust, not the love, that counts in the begetting of a child. In Joseph's case, it was the other way round. What one husband did for sexual excitement, Joseph did for spiritual fulfillment.

Here's another example of what I'm talking about here. Those men who adopt children may be said to give birth to them chastely; that's to say, in their hearts. These very same children they couldn't have begotten with their bodies.

Perhaps a look at the laws of adoption isn't out of place here, my dear Brothers and Sisters in Christ. Consider how a man becomes the son of someone who isn't his real or natural father. The stepfather acquires the rights once possessed by the father. And so it was in Joseph's case. He had the right to become a father, and with the adoption he acquired the earthly parental rights once exercised by His Heavenly Father.

In a parallel case, men generate children from women who aren't their wives; these are called natural children. Odd thing, though. The mechanics of wives and mistresses during intercourse inside and outside of marriage are remarkably the same. But where the wives take the cake is in their affection for their husbands and their marriages, not to say in their capacity for a sincerer, chaster love.

Looked at from the male point of view, the husband who could sire his children without intercourse and raise them up would be a happier man indeed, knowing that his wife didn't need the sex to love him with her whole heart.

TWO FATHERS FOR JOSEPH

Now we can address the fact that one man has not only two sons but also two fathers. Just the word "adoption" should prompt that thought. Yes, a man can have two sons, but can he really have two fathers? Well, yes, he can. One a natural father, the other an adoptive father. And so it is with Joseph.

So why do Heckle and Jeckle continue to shout their calumnies as though they were calamities? Yes, Matthew's and Luke's genealogies don't match! But the one wasn't meant to be a copy of the other. For example, as the father of Joseph, Matthew put down Jacob, and Luke put down Heli. Of course, Joseph's father could've had two names, but he didn't. And of course, these two references might indicate, if not fathers, then grandfathers or great-grandfathers or ancestors farther back than that. But somehow Joseph did have two "fathers."

That should satisfy the Heretical Hecklers! One doesn't have to be a Solomon to realize that one father could beget a child and another adopt a child. Two fathers in Christ's case having been established, is it so surprising that in a tangle of grandfathers, great-grandfathers, and other lineal descendants, two different fathers could be listed?

ADOPTION AND ADULTERY

About the law of adoption. Don't think it's foreign to our Scriptures. Don't think it's found only in civil legislation. And don't think it can't be reconciled with Divine Law. It's an ancient and honorable practice, and as such is found in ecclesiastical pronouncements going way back. Yes, insemination isn't the only source of a son; the expression of good will will do just as well. And then there's the example of wives, childless themselves, adopting their husbands' sons by their maidservants, as recorded in Genesis. Sarai asked that of Abram (16:1–4) Rachel and Leah asked that of Jacob (30:1–9). By doing their maidservants so, the men weren't committing adultery; they were only responding to the marital debt as redefined by their wives.

On this subject the Apostle Paul has something to say in his First to the Corinthians. "A wife doesn't regulate the use of her own body, but she does regulate her husband's. The same holds true for her husband" (7:4).

Moses is another example. His mother was a Hebrew, but she left him by the river in the hope that someone'd come along and give him a better life. And that's what happened, as recorded by the Exodist. He was adopted by Pharaoh's daughter (2). The Egyptian laws then weren't as the Jewish laws became; but in this instance the Pharaoh's daughter's lovely desire to adopt the Hebrew babe was considered to have the force of law. Paul again, from his to the Romans. "The Gentiles didn't have the Law as we've come to know it, but often they did things they felt were right. These were the sorts of things that later took their places in our own Law" (2:14).

Our argument seems to be this. If women can adopt, why can't men? In Genesis we read of just such an instance. Jacob was a Patriarch, the father of many children. At one point he adopted his grandchildren, the sons of his son Joseph. "I have these two as my own, with all the rights of their brothers. As for you, Joseph, your children yet to come will remain yours" (48:5–6).

Heckling and Jeckling again! The word "adoption" can't be found in Holy Scripture?

Well, the word may not appear in the Hebrew Scriptures, but that doesn't mean the reality of adoption is absent from the Scriptures. What's more, Heckle and Jeckle don't have to call Joseph adopted. I won't raise a fuss about that, provided they admit the possibility that he could also have been adopted. It goes both ways.

As for the word "adoption" in the Greek Scriptures, the Apostle Paul continually used it, and with special emphasis, when describing the Great Mystery. I mean, when Scripture made it clear that Our Lord Jesus Christ was the one and only Son of God, he described the rest of us as His adopted family with all the rights and privileges of Divine Grace. He mentioned this in his to the Galatians.

"When the fullness of time came, God the Father sent His Son to be made of a woman, made under the protection of the Law. Why? To redeem those who were under the Law. How? By adopting them" (4:4–5).

In his to the Romans he said much the same thing.

"Awaiting adoption, expecting redemption, oozing down the birth canal, we groan as though we had the staggers" (8:23).

Again in Romans he says it, with some reference to the Jews.

"As for the Jews, my brothers on this earth, I've had this nagging wish. I'd trade my own personal anathema from Christ if only He'd bless the Israelites. After all, theirs is the adoption and the glory and the Scripture and the Law. From the fleshly point of view, theirs also is Christ Himself " (9:3–5).

What's so interesting about this passage is that the practice of adoption as well as the word that describes it have both been part of Jewish history; as of course have the Scripture and the Law. And Paul put them all in the same sentence.

SONS AND FATHERS

To this very point, the Jews had another way of a natural son's becoming an adopted son. Men married the widows of their brothers who died without children. That would've kept the children within the family. You'll find it in Deuteronomy (25:5–6) and Matthew (22:24). Thus a son might be born of two fathers: his natural father and his legal father, the latter being the father from whom he'd inherit everything.

So why all this dithering about paternity? Well, no one, not even Heckle and Jeckle, should think it impossible for one man to have two fathers. And no one should think that either Matthew or Luke was playing with the truth when they constructed their genealogies of the Lord. That would just be a sacrilegious calumny, the sort that the Heretical Hecklers specialize in, the sort the Evangelists warned us against.

As for Joseph's father, Matthew listed a number of *sireds* ending in Jacob. Luke, on the other hand, could've distinguished the several types of sonship in his genealogy, but he didn't. That's to say, in Joseph's case, he could've said "Heli sired Joseph" or "Joseph whom Heli sired," but he didn't. Instead he said "Joseph son of Heli" (3:23), and of course an ambiguity was the result. Such sonship as there was came either by adoption or by the relative of a man who'd died childless and left behind a succession.

JOSEPH'S GENEALOGY, NOT MARY'S

And now, a consideration that shouldn't rock the boat.

Why are the generations counted through Joseph and not through Mary? We've said enough on that already, but to recap. She's the mother without virtue of concupiscence; he's the father without virtue of intercourse. Through him, therefore, let the generations descend or ascend. And let's not find fault with him simply because the carnal element is missing; rather let's confirm his paternity because the purity element is present.

If we didn't do this, Holy Mother Mary herself would take us by the ear! Remember, she always deferred to Joseph, especially when it came to address. "Your father and I cried our eyes out looking for You!" (Luke 2:48). Therefore, if Mary, Chastity herself, didn't find fault with Joseph, why should we let those Hecklers and Jecklers shoot off their mouths about him?

Therefore, let's count through Joseph, the chaste husband, the chaste father. Let's put Joseph over Mary according to the order of nature and the law of God. If we do it the other way around—that's to say, put Joseph in the second place and Mary in the first place—he'll cry out.

"Why did you do that? Why don't you count the generations through me, rising or descending?"

And who, pray tell, is going to be the one who'll tell Joseph, "Because you didn't pursue paternity the carnal way."

That'd allow him the riposte.

"Well, did Mary bear the child the carnal way? The Holy Spirit bears all the responsibility, or so I was led to believe, and I played my small part in it."

Joseph was a just man, the Evangelists wrote. Yes, he was just, and so was she. Respecting the Justice in both of them, then, the Holy Spirit gave the Son to both of them. He might've been born of the mother, but He was born also to the husband. That's why the Angel said, to both of them, that they had to give the child a name; if nothing else, that'd indicate their authority as parents.

For your amusement, my dear Brothers and Sisters, I give you three more such incidents of parity in parenthood.

When Zachary and Elizabeth were about to have their newborn son circumcised, they were asked the baby's name. Poor Zachary didn't have the use of his voice or ears, and so the priests turned to Elizabeth. But before she could reply, someone asked Zachary again, this time in signs. He asked for a writing tablet and wrote down the name "John" (Luke 1:60–63).

To Mary the same sentiment was expressed.

"Yes, you'll conceive a son, and you'll call his name Jesus" (Luke 1:31). "She brought forth a son to him" (Luke 2:7).

To Joseph also.

"Joseph, son of David, don't hesitate to accept Mary as your wife. Yes, she's conceived, but it's the work of the Holy Spirit. It'll be a boy, and you'll call him Jesus. Some work He'll have to do, saving the people from their sins" (Matthew 1:20–21).

In all of these instances the Gospel writers were quite certain that Joseph was the father, if not in the flesh, then in love. If that was good enough for them, then it's good enough for me.

With the greatest caution and prudence, therefore, did the Evangelists make their lists. Matthew's descending from Abraham to Christ. Luke's ascending from Christ through Abraham to God. Both through Joseph. Why? Because he was the father of Christ. And yes, it had something to do with his chastity.

"Why all this fuss about paternity?" the Hereticals shouted out? "Why don't we just all agree that Joseph did Mary the old-fashioned way and that she conceived the old-fashioned way? Why all these newfangled, far-fetched ways you just proposed? The clue here comes from Luke himself. He referred to Joseph as "a person who was generally thought to be the father of Jesus" (Luke 3:25).

Well, who'd think a thought like that? The men hanging around the corner with nothing better to do? Well, yes. After all, that's how they got their own wives in the family way. But as we know, that wasn't how it really happened with Joseph and Mary. No, the seed wasn't Joseph's, and yes, the son whom Mary bore was his as well as God the Father's, and on them all He showered love and respect.

MATTHEW DESCENDING, LUKE ASCENDING

Well, my dear Brothers and Sisters in Christ, we've answered just about every objection the Heretical Hecklers've tossed to us. Your minds should be able to rest easy now. One last question, though.

Why have the two genealogies been constructed differently? I'll tell you why. It's not easy to explain. Lord, help us understand. We're looking for some mystical meaning here.

Directionally, Matthew chose the descending route in order to signify two things. Our Lord Jesus Christ's descending to carry off our sins. His blessing all the nations descended from Abraham's seed. Of course, Matthew could've begun with Adam, the father of the whole human race, but he didn't. He could've begun with Noah after the flood; that would've included everybody on the earth; but he didn't. I suppose he could even've begun from Christ Jesus as man; that's to say, as a descendant of Adam's and the fulfillment of the prophecy about Abraham's seed; but he didn't.

Luke, on the other hand, chose the ascending route. He didn't begin at the very beginning nor at the birth of Christ but at His Baptism by John. There's some special meaning in this. Yes, the Lord used the Incarnation as an instrument by which to take away the sins of the world, and yes, He used his Baptism to atone for them.

So Matthew's descending genealogy carried the meaning of Christ's descent as the purgation of sins. Luke's ascending genealogy, as the atonement of sins not His own; that's to say, ours.

Matthew's descended through Solomon, one of David's sons; David sinned with Solomon's mother. Luke's ascended through Nathan, another of David's sons, through whom he was purged of his sin. For we've read that Nathan was sent to David, urging him to cleanse himself by doing penance (see 2 Kings 2:12).

In the person of David both genealogies, the ascending and the descending, meet. Both genealogies are the same, ascending from David to Abraham or descending from Abraham to David.

Hence, Christ, Son of David, Son of Abraham, tracks back to God. And so do we. Yes, we have to be reborn in Baptism, and our sins remitted by God.

FORTY GENERATIONS IN MATTHEW

As Matthew listed the generations, one number stuck out. Forty. A good round number. As sometimes happened in the Scriptures, the Authors didn't compute the intermediate numbers between the round ones. That was how the Scriptures described the Egyptian Captivity in Genesis (15:13) and Acts (7:6). Four hundred years. Now, to my best knowledge, it was 430 years. Be that as it may, a generation today is counted as forty years, a good usage, even though some members of that generation lived longer than forty years.

As for the use of forty years, it has at least two figurative meanings. It signifies both a lifetime of hard work here on earth and the length of time "we've been away from the Lord," as Paul put it in his Second to the Corinthians (5:6). Also it's that period of time during which the preaching of the truth is necessary.

Take the number ten. By itself it signifies beatitude in full bloom. But multiply it by four—the year has four seasons, the world has four parts—and we're back to forty again.

Forty is also a good number of days, or so the Scriptures have said, to fast. Moses did it (Deuteronomy 9:9), as did Elias (3 Kings 19:8) and indeed our own Mediator, the Lord Jesus Christ himself (Matthew 4:2). And fasting's always a good antidote, what with all the temptations that assault the body every day.

For forty years the people wandered about the desert (Numbers 32:13).

Forty days the flood lasted (Genesis 7:4).

Forty days the Risen Christ stayed with His friends, chatting up the Resurrection (Acts 1:3).

In this last instance "forty" indicates how long we've been away from God and intimates how we should make good use of the time between now and His return. We can best do that by commemorating the Lord's Body, which is what we do in church, as Paul said in his First to the Corinthians (11:26).

Yes, Our Lord descended to this life and, yes, the Word was made flesh, all that He might be delivered up for our sins and, after our justification, that He might rise again, as Paul put it to the Romans (4:25) In all this, forty's the number Matthew followed. Forty's the number of years, whether more or less, for a generation. Four hundred's the number of years, more or less, for the Egyptian captivity.

As for the forty generations in Matthew's genealogy—down from forty-two to make a round number—is still a good number, even if we add Our Lord to make forty-one. But He was man, and He was God, and hence perhaps He shouldn't be included in the count. Why? Well, there've been many a holy man and many a wise man, but there's never been one of whom it could be said, as the Evangelist John did, "The Word was made flesh" (1:14).

SEVENTY-SEVEN GENERATIONS IN LUKE

Luke, on the other hand, using an ascending order, had seventy-seven entries in his genealogy. Beginning with the Baptism of Our Lord Jesus Christ, he ascended through Joseph and through Adam until He reached God. His rationale behind this was that seventy-seven was the mystical number of times a person's sins should be forgiven. That'd include the remission of all the sins that takes place at Baptism.

For the Lord, of course, Baptism was a symbolic event; that's to say, He hadn't committed any sins that needed forgiving. But in His humility, by undergoing the Baptism Himself, He recommended its usefulness to the rest of us.

And for the rest of the Trinity too. Present at, and indeed in, the Jordan River with the Son were the Father and the Holy Spirit. It was a sort of consecration of the Son's Baptism, and consequently of the Baptism of all future Christians. How were the Holy Three present? The Father's voice came down from Heaven. The Son in the form of a Mediator. The Holy Spirit in the form of a dove. Or so Matthew reported (3:16–17).

THE NUMBER SEVENTY-SEVEN

I think I need to put a finer point on an argument I've just used. Seventy-seven, as I said, was the number of sins that are forgiven in Baptism. I'm not quite sure, but a reasonable explanation would run something like this.

The number ten has the perfection of Justice and Beatitude. But only when the creature, signified by the number seven, clings to its Creator; an example of this would be the Catalog of the Law consecrated in ten precepts. A transgression of any of the ten is signified by the number eleven; a transgression was defined as a sin against Justice whereby a man sought something that wasn't his. A good definition, this; or at least Paul thought so. In his First to Timothy, he called such avarice the root of all evils (6:10). The Psalmist has called sin a form of fornication in that it separates the soul from the Lord (VUL 72:27; NRSV 73:27). All of which is to say, there's something plaintive about a sin, and something plaintive about the Lord's response to a soul that wanders. "It's as though He'd hoped to find something rather more."

More about the sinner and the sin. The sinner wants to rejoice in his privacy; that's to say, he separates the things that are Jesus Christ's from the things that are his own—Paul had something to say about this in his to the Philippians (2:21)—and the Charity "that doesn't seek what's rightfully hers," as Paul put it in his First to the Corinthians (13:5), is praised.

As I said, eleven, the number signifying transgression, when multiplied, not by ten, but by seven, equals seventy-seven.

Transgression has less to do with the Trinity of the Creator than it does with the creaturely sinner himself, who is signified by the number seven. Three for his soul coming from the Three-ness of the Creator in whose image he was made. Four for his body, which is made up of the four elements: fire, air, earth, water. There's no need for everyone to know what they are. It's somewhat easier just to look at the world as though it were a body. Easiest of all is just to look at our own bodies as we move about from one place to another in four directions, all mentioned in Scripture: East, West, South, and North.

Sins, as you've no doubt noticed, my dear Brothers and Sisters, have two sources. Either they're prompted by movements of the soul—that's to say, by acts of the will not visible to the naked eye—or by acts of the body that are all too visible to the naked eye. It was these images that preoccupied the prophet Amos (1,2). He pictured God as making threatening gestures and saying threatening things. "For a bundle of impieties I'll turn you out, have no doubt about that! But for just three or four, perhaps I won't. Whatever happens, you won't mistake Me when I do it."

To sum up. A person is the sum of two numbers: three for the nature of the soul; four for the nature of the body.

AT THE END AS AT THE BEGINNING—THE SCRIPTURES

So eleven times seven equals seventy-seven. Seventy-seven has to do with a transgression of Justice that makes the sinner a very lonely person indeed. Seventy-seven is the sum of all the sins that are remitted at and through Baptism. Seventy-seven generations in Luke's genealogy, indicating that man is reconciled with God through the abolition of all the sins. Seventy-seven times, at least according to the Evangelist Matthew, Peter is supposed to forgive a brother who offends (18:22).

There are many more hidden treasures among the mysteries of God, but they'll have to be flushed out, and indeed fleshed out, by more diligent and worthy fellows than me.

I've done about the best I can on this difficult subject. The Lord helped, the lack of time didn't. Any one of you present here today may well know more than I. But don't knock on my door to tell me. It's the Lord's door you should be thumping. Yes, He was my inspiration too.

One last thing to keep in mind. Don't be alarmed by the Holy Scriptures as a whole! When you come across a passage that doesn't make sense, don't keep it a secret. When you finally do make sense out of it, don't crow about it. All of which is to say, when you can't make heads or tails out of a passage, you should still defer to its Wisdom. And when you finally do know which is heads and which tails, do use this Wisdom with all possible Charity.

SERMONS

TO THE

PEOPLE

ADVENT, **CHRISTMAS**,

NEW YEAR'S, EPIPHANY

2

SERMO CLXXXIV

Christmas #1

MAKING SENSE OUT OF THE
INCARNATION

This is the birthday of Our Lord and Savior
Jesus Christ! This is also the day that Truth
rose out of the earth, as the Psalmist put it
(VUL 84:12; NRSV 85:11)! And this is the day the
Day of Days was born!

As the anniversary rolls around each
year, this happiest of days must be celebrated
by us. And so we do, exulting and rejoicing
as the Psalmist did on so many similar occasions (VUL 117:24; NRSV 118:24)!

Yes, it's a sublime moment, dizzying
really, but yet it's also fraught with humility.
At least that's the story our Christian faith
tells. Yet what seems so close to us seems so
far from the hearts of others. They're the

ones who pride themselves on knowledge of the world. They're the ones who think deviously and act cagily, and wouldn't be caught dead doing a pious act. It's from these poor folk God has hidden the wonders of His Incarnation.

Yes, He's hidden them from the adult but childish people who rule so much of our daily lives. But yet He's revealed them in all their glory, as Matthew told us in his Gospel, to the childlike among us, old and young (11:25). Therefore, let the humble tend their humility. Soon enough the asinine in their lives will turn to aquiline; that's to say, their infirmities will take flight to God's highest perch.

About those so-called wise and prudent people, I have a further word. They leisurely entertain stylish, sophistical queries about God, yes, but they don't spend a lot of time on the fond if sometimes foolish tasks and trials of the spiritual life. They think these trifles beneath their contempt, they brush them aside. But in this they make a terrible miscalculation. By making a clean sweep of the trash around them, they'd soon discover the treasure that's well within their reach.

Who are these people anyway? Well, they're the Empty-headed and the Light-hearted, the Deflated and the Inflated. And how will we know them? Well, they dangle somewhere between Heaven and Earth, on that lofty plain, perhaps, where the Blowhards blow their best—or should I say, their worst?

Yes, they have the Wisdom and Prudence of this world. But why is it that they have nothing to do with the Person by whom this world was made in the first place? If ever there were a whiff of true Wisdom in their flatulent remarks, they'd understand that Christ couldn't have been changed into human flesh; that human flesh is merely a garment; and that it could only have been donned by Christ.

They'd understand also that He assumed what He wasn't, all the while remaining what He was; that He'd come to us in Humankind's clothing while at the same time He hadn't left His Father's closet; that

He'd never left that holy state while He was appearing to us as we were; that heavenly power was added to an infant body, and yet the earth's resources weren't any the poorer. On the one hand, Christ's task while remaining in the presence of the Father is the whole earth. On the other hand, His task while coming among us was the birthing of the Virgin.

To be sure, this was Majesty, as it might variously be defined. The Virgin Mother, as much a virgin before conception as after parturition, gave some indication of it. She was found pregnant by a man, her husband, but not made pregnant by him, her husband or any other man. She grew heavy with a male child without a male adult having to lie heavily on her to beget that child. She grew happier as her fecundity increased without at the same time having her virginity decreased.

So what do the so-called Wise and Prudent think of this great miracle? Well, they prefer to think of it as a nice story rather than a hard fact. So when it comes to Christ appearing as man and God—clearly a divine consideration—they run into trouble. They think it beneath them to believe that there are things that aren't human; that there are in fact things that are divine. Hence, they see no reason why they can't condemn the existence of the divine altogether. To them it's just plain embarrassing that God should walk around in a funny, ill-fitting body. To us, of course, it's a greatly encouraging sight. To put it another way, which'll truly appear perverse to the Unwise and Imprudent, the more impossible the virgin birth of a human being appears to them, the more divine it seems to us.

MAKING SENSE FOR ALL PRESENT

So, let's celebrate the birthday of Our Lord with all due frequency and festivity. It does set dancing, men and women! Christ was born a man, borne from a woman's womb; male and female, who should take more credit for this wonderful event? Fortunately for both sexes, there is more than enough praise to go round.

Now, let's pass to my next point. The Second Man, who was around at the beginning and then was damned; that's to say, Adam.

Persuading Adam to do what he shouldn't have, a woman brought death upon him and hence upon us. Yet it was a woman, this very same sex, who brought forth life to us. As Paul wrote to the Romans, it was a God who assumed "what we assumed was our flesh, the first sin also included" (8:3). It was He who, when born, cleansed the flesh of that sin. It wasn't that the flesh had befouled itself so much as that the sin had died so that nature might live. How did that happen? There was born Someone without sin, and in that Someone the sinner was born again and again and again.

Therefore, who's really got the right to rejoice?

Yes, you, you holy young men in the monastery! When you could be out pursuing marriage, you're inside following Christ. You don't have to do it this way, of course, but it's been your own special choice. As for Himself, He didn't come to you through marriage, but you don't seem to count that against Him. That's to say, you don't feel you have to think poorly of marriage, a necessary human institution if there ever was one, but you could. After all, you're all the result of carnal nuptials; but Christ was the end result of spiritual nuptials. No wonder, then, that human marriage has lost its appeal for you. If, in fact, Christ had been born your way, then you probably wouldn't be loving Him so much today.

And yes, you holy young women in the convent, you too should also rejoice! Why? The Virgin of Virgins has brought forth a man with whom you can willingly enjoy the wonderfulness of matrimony without at the same time endangering the strength of your virginity. Neither by conceiving Him nor by bearing Him can you lose that quality that first made Him take a second look at you; that's to say, your love, your uncommitted love, your virginity.

And you folk for whom Justice has had a special meaning should also rejoice—it's the birthday of Justice Himself!

And you who suffer from chronic fatigue and disease should re- joice—this is the birthday of the Divine Physician!

And you captives and hostages should rejoice—this is the birthday of the One who'll ransom you from your captivity!

And you slaves should rejoice too—it's your Master's birthday!

And you freemen—it's the birthday of your Emancipator!

Yes, all you Christians here this morning should rejoice—it's Christ's birthday!

MAKING SENSE OUT OF TWO NATIVITIES

What can I say?

Christ was born of a human mother and hence has commended that holy day to the ages. He was born of a Divine Father and hence has created all the ages. That nativity never had a mother, nor can this nativity we're celebrating today ever seek the help of a father.

What else can I say?

Christ was born of a father and a mother, but without a father or a mother. That's to say, as God He was born of a Father; as man, of a mother. Without a mother He's still a Divine Being; without a father He's still a human being. How? It's something of a conundrum. As Isaiah put it, how can one describe His generation? Who'll make any sense out of it? (53:8)

One generation is outside the seam of time; the other is without the semen of time. The one is without a beginning; the other without a parallel. The one that always was and never wasn't; the other that had no precedent or succedent. The one that doesn't end; another that does indeed have a beginning and an ending.

Deservedly, therefore, did the Prophets announce He'd be born; the Heavens and the Angels, that He'd been born. He lay in a manger, and yet the world rested in his hands. As an infant, He was wordless, and yet He was the Word Itself. Him whom the Heavens couldn't huddle, the lap of a single woman could easily cuddle. She was toting about on her hip Him Who carries her about the universe. Her breasts were running, but they were enriching the Bread of Life.

How the High has come so low! How Divinity has crept into humanity! The mother on whom the Infant was so dependent was so dependent on Him, the Ruler of the Universe. Her whose breasts He was suckling, He'd already been nourishing with Truth. He didn't shrink from assuming our primordials, nor should we abhor donning His celestials. He wished to become one of our children in order to do something lovely for us; that's to say, make us all His children, the children of God.

3

SERMO CLXXXV

Christmas #2

SPRINGING FROM THE EARTH

When the Wordiness of an Other-wordly
God revealed itself as a wordly if wordless
tot, and when the Word of God let out, if not
the Wisdom of God, then an unholy howl—
that's when we're talking about the Birthday
of the Lord.

The Scholars in the East read the Divine
Event in the skies. The Shepherds in the hills
heard the Angelic Voices. We get the word
today, the anniversary of the event, in the
solemnity of our celebration. In it we refer to
the Psalmist's prophecy. "Truth has sprung
from the earth, and Justice has looked down
from Heaven" (VUL 84:12; NRSV 85:11).

Yes, the Truth that's in the Father's

breast has sprung from the earth to be at the same time at the bosom of His mother.

The Truth that holds the world together with rugged hands has sprung from the earth so that He may be held by His mother's lacey fingers.

The Truth from which the Angels sip has sprung from the earth so that it may suck milk from His mother's breasts.

The Truth that overflows the Heavens' banks has sprung from the earth so that it may lie within the friendly confines of a manger.

When Sublimity cloaked itself with Subtlety like this, who stands to gain? Well, there's no dividend here to the Divine Treasury that I can see. Apparently, if we have any faith at all, we're the sole beneficiaries.

Hence, Humanity, this is a wake-up call for you! God's becoming a human being is for your advantage alone.

"Rise up, you who're still dead asleep," as Paul shouted to the Ephesians, "and Christ'll sweep the sleepers from your eyes" (5:14).

It was for you, my dear Brothers and Sisters, that God was made man. If He hadn't been born in our time, you'd still be sleeping the sleep of death. If He hadn't donned the same fatal flesh that Adam had, you'd never have been liberated from the sin of the flesh. If this Mercy hadn't happened to you, Perpetual Misery would possess you whole and entire. If He hadn't come to die the death for you, you wouldn't have been born again. If He hadn't propped you up, you'd have flopped yourselves down. Quite simply put, if He hadn't come, you'd be dead as a doornail.

HANDING DOWN THE GIFT

Let's be joyful and celebrate the advent of our Salvation and Redemption!

Let's celebrate the feast day, the day on which the Great and Eternal Day made His appearance in our Brief and Passing Day!

As Paul put it in his First to the Corinthians, "Here on earth, just for us, He was made into Justice and Sanctification, and Redemption. It reminds me of Jeremiah. 'He who feels like glorying, should do his glorying in the Lord' (9:23)" (1:30–31).

"We shouldn't do as the Jews did, adopt an attitude of pride." As Paul described it to the Romans (10:3), they "didn't know the Justice of God and didn't feel subject to it; hence, they wanted to set up a Justice System of their own."

But when the Psalmist sang "Truth has sprung out of the earth," he quickly added that "Justice has looked down upon the earthly scene." He did so because he didn't want mere mortality to rule our roost. Nor did he want Humankind to make these statements on its own. Nor did he want Humankind to justify itself, believing it had the power to do so itself. In other words, the Psalmist didn't want Humankind to trash God's Justice System.

Some variations on this theme.

"Truth has sprung from the earth," sang the Psalmist.

"I'm the Truth," said the Christ (John 14:6), and He was born of a virgin.

"Justice has looked down upon the scene" because Humankind believes, not in itself, but in Him who was born, and feels justified in doing so.

"Truth has sprung from the earth." Why? "The Word was made flesh" (John 1:14), that's why. "And Justice has looked down and seen an eyeful." Why? Well, at least according to James, "every classy present, every perfect gift, has been handed down from Heaven" (1:17).

"The Truth has sprung from the earth." The flesh has sprung from Mary.

"And Justice has looked down upon the scene from Heaven

above." Why? "There'd be no gift for a human to accept if Heaven hadn't already handed it down" (John 3:27).

IF NO GRACE, THEN NO HOPE

"May those who've been justified by faith look peacefully upon God through Our Lord Jesus Christ," wrote Paul in his to the Romans. "It's through Him that we have access to such grace as we have, and through Him that we'll have such glory in the hope of God" (5:1–2).

Some ruminations from the heart.

Let's place these words of the Apostle over against some words from the Psalmist. Compare Paul's "having received faith from God, let's return the favor to God," with the Psalmist's "coming along the road from different directions, Justice and Peace saw each other at a distance and ran to each other with open arms" (VUL 84:11; NRSV 85:10).

Let's also meditate on Paul's words "through our Lord Jesus Christ." Why? Because "Truth has sprung out of the earth. And it is through Justice Himself that we have access to such grace as we possess and such glory as we'll have in the hope of God."

Notice the Apostle didn't say "our glory"; he said "the glory of God." Why? Because "Justice" doesn't come from within; "it comes down from Heaven."

"The person who glories will glory" not in himself—what a waste that'd be—but "in the glory of the Lord."

That's why the Angelic Voice heralded the birth of the Lord from a virgin—"Glory to God in the highest, and peace to men of good will in the lowest" (Luke 2:14)—and that's why we celebrate the birthday of the Lord today.

Where did "peace on earth" come from? From "the Truth that sprang from the earth; that's to say, from Christ who was born of the flesh. As Paul wrote to the Ephesians, "He's our peace; He's the one who brought both Heaven and earth together" (2:14). He wanted them to be good persons bound to each other with the sure if silken cords of unity.

In that grace, wrote Paul in his Second to the Corinthians (1:12) let's rejoice that our glory will be an indication of our conscience. That way we'll glory not in ourselves but in the Lord.

Hence, it was said by the Psalmist, "You hold my feet to the ground—You raise my head to the sky" (VUL 3:4; NRSV 3:3).

What greater grace of God could have illumined us? God had a Son Himself and made Him the son of man. And also the other way around. God had a son and made him the Son of God?

Great questions arise from our shallow hearts.

Don't I have some just desserts coming?

There's a problem, yes, but aren't I part of the solution?

At the Final Assize won't God err in my favor, give me some slack?

Is there no hope at all?

"Not really" would seem to be the answer, except perhaps for the grace of the Incarnation.

4

SERMO CLXXXVI

Christmas #3

WHO'S LIVING WHERE?

Let's rejoice, my Brothers and Sisters!

A happy day it is for us as well as for the nations of the world!

This particular day has been made special not by the sun we see but by its Creator whom we can't see. When did that happen? When a Virgin Mother poured forth from her fertility, without the aid of her genitalia, Him whom we could see. All that was made possible by her Creator whom we can't see.

Yes, she remained a virgin during it all. A virgin conceiving. A virgin birthing! A virgin while heavy with child. A virgin after she'd delivered the child. A virgin forever!

Why then, O Humankind, do you roll

your eyes at that? When God thought it worth His while to become a Human Being, He did just that. That's to say, that was the way He was born.

He'd already made her what she was. Why then couldn't she make Him what He turned out to be?

Before He was made a human being, He already was God, yes. And yes, after He was made a human being, He lost none of His strength.

Another perspective.

While still with His heavenly Father, He made Himself an earthly Mother. While still in His heavenly home, He took up residence in the womb of His mother.

How could God become less than God? That's to ask, how could the Supreme Being be left in the lurch when He became a human being?

He honored his mother by allowing her to retain her virginity when she gave birth.

When the Word was made flesh, it didn't mean that He could no longer be the Word. Rather it meant just the opposite. The flesh, if it was ever going to survive, approached the Word for fear it'd die. That's to say, a human being has body and soul; Christ is a Supreme Being and a Human Being. There's the God who's a man, and who's also God while being a man.

Does all this sound like an aberration in the natural course of things? No, it's just the unity of person.

A final consideration.

If all this is so, mayn't we say that humanity was added to the divinity of Christ? Doesn't that now mean a fourth resident has joined the Trinity? Alas, no further additions to the divine residence. No guest rooms within the present residence. The Trinity is quite comfortable as They are, thank you very much.

MORE IS LESS, LESS IS MORE

There are people with short attention spans who nonetheless express their opinions long and loud. We've heard what they have to say about such things as the Rule of Faith and the sayings of the Divine Scriptures. To these Heretical Hecklers you listen at your risk.

For example, they say things like this. "The person who's the son of man has become the Son of God; but the Son of God didn't reciprocate; that's to say, didn't become the son of man."

To think this up, Heckle and Jeckle had to sit still long enough to learn what was true and what wasn't. But apparently not long enough to be able to have a decent conversation about the truth. How's that? Well, they studied all right—I'll give them that—but only half the question. They readied themselves on how Human Nature could be changed for the better, but they paid no attention to how Divine Nature could be changed for the worse.

Well, here's the truth, the whole truth.

The Word was made flesh, yes, but Divinity was none the worse for the transaction. We have Scripture's word for this. It doesn't say the flesh was made Word; John said just the opposite. "The Word was made flesh" (1:14). Why? "God is the Word" (1:1). What's "flesh" after all but being a human being, with everything that implies. That's how Matthew expressed it in his whole Gospel; one reference should do it. "His soul was sad to the point of death" (26:38).

If therefore the Word is God and the man is flesh, then what can "the Word was made flesh" mean but that God was made man? From that it follows that the Son of God was made the Son of Man all right, but not by taking on something worse or taking on something better; but by adding something without at the same time subtracting anything.

Our confession in the Rule of Faith—to believe in the Son of God who was born of the Virgin Mary—what kind of vigor would that statement have if in reality only the son of man, and not the Son of God, was born of the Virgin Mary? What Christian would deny that the son of man was born from that woman? That God was made man, and so man was made God? Our proof. "God was made Word, and the Word, flesh."

Therefore, it has to be confessed that He who was the Son of God, in order to be born of the Virgin Mary, had to dump His divinity before He could don His humanity. Remaining what He was, He assumed what He wasn't; that's to say, He disguised His divinity for something rather less than the Father, without at the same time losing any of His identity with the Father.

PICKING A BIRTHDAY

If He who's always Son of God didn't become son of man, then the Apostle Paul was in a tight spot in his to the Philippians.

"When He was the Son of God, He didn't think it demeaning to be equal to God the Father. But then He went and took the form of a slave, dumping His divinity in the process. That's to say, He looked like a man, He walked like a man, He talked like a man. So what could I conclude but that He was a man" (2:6–7).

No, there was no stand-in. We have the right Person. He's God, He's equal to the Father, He's the only begotten son of the Father. So why did He go and dump His divinity in order to take on His humanity. No substitute here. No surrogate. "He humbled," not someone else, not a bystander, not a stranger, but "Himself, setting Himself on a track that'd end only in death—ahem—the death of the cross." How could the Son of God have done this except as the son of man?

Another perspective.

Again, if the Son of God didn't become the son of man at least for a while, how could the Apostle Paul make this colossal statement to the Romans?

"Quite apart from the Gospel of God, and indeed before there were such things as Gospels, God the Father promised, through his Prophets, as recorded in the Holy Scriptures, that His Son'd appear, made from the seed of David according to the flesh" (1:1–3).

If that statement wasn't true, then Paul was a fountain of misinformation!

But here He is again, the Son of God, as He always was, made from the seed of David according to the flesh—something that'd never happened before.

Another perspective.

In the unlikely event that the Son of God didn't become the son of man, then how, as Paul wrote to the Galatians, "did God send His Son to be born of a woman?" (4:4). Please note that this noun "woman," as it appears in the Hebrew language, indicates respect to the virginal as well as the nonvirginal; that's to say, it represents the feminine sex.

To return, whom did the Father send but His only begotten Son? How, therefore, was He "born of a woman" unless He was sent to become the son of man?

Yes, He was born of the Father before time was ticked off into days. Now that there are days, there are also weeks and years, and today's the anniversary of the event that we're celebrating today.

Why did He create this day on which He Himself would be created from a mother whom He Himself had already created?

It's as good a day as any. The Winter Solstice. Fall changing into winter. The shortest day. With each succeeding day the light becomes longer—couldn't this signify the work of Christ?

Day by day, according to Paul in his Second to the Corinthians (4:16), the interior man becomes stronger.

Is it any wonder, then, why the Timeless Timekeeper should pick this day in time to be the birthday of His Son made man?

5

SERMO CLXXXVII

Christmas #4

WORD GAMES

"Open my lips, O Lord, so that my voice
may break out in praise!" So the Psalmist has
sung (VUL 50:17; NRSV 51:15). He was saluting
his Lord with a chain of seemingly incom-
patible attributes. And so too I sing this
morning.

Almighty God the Father I want to praise
but, to my amazement, He's the Infant
Christ.

The Lord has made all things, and yet He
takes His stand among the very things He's
made.

He's the Revealer of His Father, and at the
same time He's the Creator of His mother.

He's the Son of God born of the Father

without a mother; and He's the son of man born of a mother without a father.

He's the Day as the Angels count time; He's the Clock as human beings tick off the day.

He's the Word of God before there were timepieces; He's the Word made flesh who stopped the clock when He was made flesh.

He made the sun with His own hands, and yet He Himself was made under the light and heat of the sun.

He regulates human history from the bosom of His Father; and yet He consecrates this one particular day from the womb of His mother.

He remains with His Father, and yet He goes forth from His mother.

He's the Creator of the heavens and the earth; and yet He takes His own rise under the heavens, that's to say from the earth.

As God He has more Wisdom than He can mouth, and yet as a babe He hasn't enough mouth to utter the Wisdom He knows.

He fills the world with jots and tittles, and yet He Himself lies a tot in a manger.

He sets the stars in motion, and yet he sucks His mother's breasts.

He's so great as a god, yet so small as a slave.

His divinity isn't underwhelmed by His humanity, nor is His humanity overwhelmed by His divinity.

He didn't abandon His divine agenda when He picked up His carpenter's tools.

He didn't stop holding His universe together with His mighty arms while He was trying to catch flies with His baby fingers. A borrowing, more or less, from the Book of Wisdom (8:1).

He put on the clumsiness of the flesh when He entered the Virgin's womb, and yet His movement throughout the universe wasn't hampered by the baggy pants.

He didn't take away the food of Wisdom from the Angels while He was supplying us with the sweetness of the Lord.

THERE AND HERE

Well, what's so remarkable about a stay-at-home Word-of-God who sometimes travels?

Perhaps the best way to handle this question is to use a comparison, comparing the Word of God with a sermon about the Word of God.

Here I am in the middle of that sermon, what with my arms flailing about, my words flying around. Everyone hears what I'm saying; that's to say, my words go in the one ear and out the other. But unless my words stop in your head long enough to be heard, they don't do either of us any good.

Of course, if I whispered them into your ear, then only one person could hear them, and the rest of you couldn't. But that's not the point I'm trying to make.

Clearly this sermon as a whole has many parts; it's divided into words, and the longer words, into syllables. But when I speak, all you hear is the sermon as a whole.

Coincidentally but importantly, each one of you hears the whole thing. Which is another way of saying that you, whether as a group or an individual, can't choose not to hear some of the words, some of the syllables.

A good sermon—if I may be permitted a comparison within a comparison—isn't like a good dinner where you can pick and choose. *The squash, yes, but not the squid!* In other words, you have to hear the whole thing, eat the whole thing, whether you like it or not.

Now while I'm sermonizing, having this conversation with you about the nativity of the Lord, I don't sit up here and worry about whether only one of you hears the sermon, leaving the rest of you with nothing to hear. That'd be ridiculous! What I really worry about is defrauding your mind's ear. That's to say, I want you—all of you and each of you—to be attentive enough to hear the whole sermon.

But how does that work?

One theory has it, as I've already hinted, that the sermon enters your ears first, stops for a while, then leaves your ears in order to enter-stop-leave somebody else's ears, and so on *seriatim* around the church.

As is obvious even to the dullest among us, that makes no sense. This sermon hits all of you and each of you, but at one and the same time. Yet, it's for all of you to appreciate as if you were the only one in the church.

Thus the comparison once begun comes full circle. The Word of God has always been as much with the Father in Heaven as He is in my sermon on the Word of God today.

And if I may carry the comparison one step further, the Word of God Himself as He dwells in my sermon is as much with you today, whether as a group or as an individual, as He's always been with the Father in Heaven.

In other words, the Word of God can indeed travel, without having to surrender His one true home.

What's so remarkable is that He actually did it once and continues to do it!

CHANGING AND UNCHANGING

Therefore, no one should believe the Son of God was converted or transmuted into the son of man. Rather we should believe that He remained the Son of God even while He was being made the son of man; that's to say, without a loss of divine substance but with a gain of human substance.

When John the Evangelist said "God is the Word" and "the Word was made flesh" (1:1,14), he was describing a theological reality. What these words don't mean is that in the process God ceased to be. What they do mean is that Emmanuel was born; that's to say, the "Emmanuel, God with us" that Matthew spoke of (1:25).

So much for the scriptural argument. Now for the philosophical one.

The word we carry in our heart becomes the word we speak when it pops from our mouth. But the word itself isn't really changed to voice; it isn't actually affected by the process of speaking. If anything, it's enriched by the process. That's to say, what's heartfelt remains but also gets expressed outside the heart.

And just the opposite is true. What's been heard outside is just the same as what's heartfelt within. When the word becomes voice, it isn't changed into voice. To the hearer it sounds like a word just spoken, yes, but to the thinker at the same time it's spoken, it doesn't leave the thinker in the lurch; that's to say, it hasn't deserted the thinker.

The spoken word is thought of in silence—it could be a Greek or Latin word or a word from some other language—but that's not what I have in mind here. What I have in mind is the sentiment the word expresses. The moment before it's said in whatever language, it resides, so to speak, in the lexicon of the heart of the one thinking it; it's innocent of any language till it's spoken out loud in the voice and language of the speaker.

However, both of these—what's thought by the intellect, and what's said in the speech—are changeable and exchangeable. For example, neither'll remain when you forget it; and both'll be gone when you're silent. The Word of God, on the other hand, remains steady as He goes and entertains no change in course.

EXTEMPORIZING

What the Lord was doing might best be described as extemporizing, assuming the flesh as He did. That's when He made His entrance into this life. You might think He'd have lost some eternity by this reckless act, but He didn't. Rather He seems to have gained some immortality for the flesh.

And so He Himself appeared, as the Psalmist put it (VUL 18:16; NRSV 19:16) "as the bridegroom bounding out of the bridal chamber after a night of joy; like the marathoner who'd left the pack behind and finished the race with nobody in sight!"

Paul put it this way in his to the Philippians. "While He was in the form of God He didn't think it indecent to be equal to God" (2:6).

To help us He became what He wasn't, said Paul in the next verse. "He emptied Himself," not denting the form of God so much as "donning the form of a slave," and through this new form "He was made in the likeness of men." That's to say, He didn't look like God; He looked like man (2:7).

Yes, we're the sum of our parts, whether in soul or body; that's our nature. And that's what He put on. It makes us what we are. Of course, if Christ weren't one of us, He'd still be God. But when all this Incarnation business began, He continued to be God. But, I must tell you, He wasn't just one of us; He was also one of them, that's to say, the Trinity.

According to John, He was made man, yes, "for the Father is greater than I" (14:28); and He remained God, "I and the Father are the one and the same" (10:30).

For if the Word-into-flesh, that's to say, God, is condensed into man, that statement—"the Father is greater than I"—wouldn't ring true. God and man aren't one and the same; God is higher. Nor would it be true to say that "I and the Father are one and the same." Why? Because God and man aren't one and the same.

Perhaps He can say, I and the Father, we aren't one and the same, but once upon a time we were. For what He was He's stopped being; that's to say, He isn't today what He was yesterday.

Now however, because He can be mistaken for a slave, He can truly say, "The Father's greater than I." Because He can be recognized in the true form of God, which is His permanent status, He can truly say, without a trace of whimsy, "I and the Father are one and the same."

Therefore, when He arrived among humanity, He dumped His divinity, not so much for the delight of a change, but to highlight the exchange. That's to say, dimming down what He was, a God, He was able to reveal what He'd become, a slave. As Isaiah has said, "A boy was born to us" (9:6).

The Word of God, who remains in eternity, became flesh that "He might live in and among us." That was made possible by His dimming down, His dumbing down, His hanging around. As Gabriel trumpeted His name, so we call Him by this name, "Emanuel." Becoming man, remaining God, He may rightly be called "God with us." That means, we don't call one of them God and the other one, man.

So after all this sermonizing, may the world rejoice in those who believe all this!

To save these lucky folk, He came through the one the world had made.

The Creator of Mary is also the Son of Mary.

The Son of David and the Lord of David.

The seed of Abraham before there was an Abraham.

Maker of the earth and made on earth.

Creator of the heavens and created under the sky.

He's "the day the Lord has made" (Psalm VUL 117:24; NRSV 118:24).

"He's the light of my heart" (VUL Canticle of Canticles, 3:11; NRSV Song of Solomon, 3:11).

Let's stroll in the light of His aura!

Let's rejoice in His presence!

Let's be truly glad He's here with us today, of all days!

6

SERMO CLXXXVIII

Christmas #5

SIRING AND BEING SIRED

We should praise the Son of God, as He's coequal and co-eternal with the Father. He's the Contractor of everything built in Heaven and on Earth, the structures as well as the infrastructures, the Word of God and God Himself, the life and light of Humankind.

But no amount of sermonizing could do Justice to that. For how can our language praise with dignity and strength Him whom our heart can't really see? It's the cataracts, the iniquities, that blind us. May our poor vision on earth improve! As the Evangelist Matthew has said, may our eyes clear up so that we may see God in Heaven (5:8).

It's not much of a surprise, I say, that we

can't find the proper words with which to express the One True Word, let alone our response to it.

These words I'm speaking to you now were formed in my mind first. Prior to that, my mind was formed by that very same Word. But there's a difference here. Man doesn't make words in the same way that He was formed through the Word. That's because the Father didn't beget the Unique Word in the same way that He made everything else through the Word. Siring and being sired, making and being made, generating and being generated—however you want to describe that furious activity, God is and remains one.

However, God made the world. The world passes, comes and goes, and God remains. As for all the created stuff, it didn't generate itself. It wasn't made by anyone visible, that's for certain. Nor was the Invisible Creator of all the stuff made by anyone visible.

It isn't so surprising, then, when Human Beings—themselves some of the stuff that's been made—can't find the words to explain the Invisible Word through whom all that stuff was made in the first place.

FOR WHOSE SAKE WAS IT?

Mulling over Scripture verses is always a worthwhile thing to do. "In the beginning was the Word, and the Word was with God, and the Word was God"—this is the type of passage I have in mind. But I'd rather look at the words "the Word was made flesh." Do we perhaps speak about Him only because, as the Evangelist John put it, "He spent some time among us"? (1:1,14). Or only because we could see Him when He was among us?

Speaking about Him—that's how we celebrate this day, the day of days on which He thought it worth His while to be born of a Virgin. Such a story!

God was born of God in eternity, or so Isaiah wrote (53:8), "but who'll tell that story?" In eternity there is no day for solemnizing or celebrating an event or indeed anything else. Sunset, sunrise—there is none. One year followed by another year, there is none. Indeed there's no change, just that Unique Word of God, Who's turned out to be the life, the light of Humankind, the long blue Eternal Day.

But there was a day within our short blue Day. The day on which He, joined to human flesh, flashed "from the wedding chamber like a bridegroom." That day is now. Not tomorrow. Truly today extols His emergence from the Virgin—that's what makes this day holy.

What praises shall we make, what thanks shall we give to the Charity of God?

It was because of us—that's why He came from where there was no time to become a timepiece for us.

An oldster before the world had whiskers, He nonetheless became a youngster for us.

He became what He used to create, a human being.

He created His mother whom He'd already created.

He was toted about as a tot in the very hands He'd already shaped into hands.

He drew milk from the very breasts He'd already filled.

While a wordless tot in the manger, the Word whimpered like a babe—and this is the Word without whom human eloquence would be just a squeak, a squawk!

OBEYING AND NOT OBEYING

Today, O Humankind, see what God has become for you! Acknowledge the lesson of such humongous humility, taught by a Teacher who hasn't learned to speak!

All Humankind, once there was a time when you were so facile and creative with words that you gave a name to every living creature in Paradise (Genesis 2:19–20). But now, because of you, Your Creator lies a speechless tot and can't for the life of Him call His mother by name.

When you brooded on a broad preserve bursting with fruit trees as far as the eye could see, you perished. You starved to death because you didn't know the value of obedience. But the Son of Man knew, when He came as a mortal into the narrowest, most cramped, meanest, most tumbledown, ramshackled outbuilding of a run-down, fleabag caravanserai. It was you He was looking for, for He wanted to save you by dying Himself. You're human beings, yes, but you wanted to be God; the result was that you died the death (Genesis 3).

On the other hand, He was God, but wanted to become man. He wanted to find out what our casualty figures truly were. Catastrophic! Human Pride had pressed us so flat that only Divine Humility could raise us up.

VIRGINITY UNDAMAGED

Therefore, my dear Brothers and Sisters, let's celebrate with joyful heart this day on which Mary bore the Savior. She was promised in marriage to the Creator of marriage. She was a virgin conjoined to the Prince of virgins. She was given to a husband, and she was a mother without virtue of her husband. A virgin before marriage, a virgin during marriage. A virgin in expectation, a virgin in lactation. But all that was only to be expected. When her Omnipotent Son was born, He didn't damage her virginity in the birthing process; after all, He chose her as He was about to be born.

On the fertility scale marriage rates the highest. But on the holiness scale virginity ranks the highest. Therefore, the man Christ, who's distinguished as both God and man, would never give Mary the gift that husbands and wives enjoy. Rather He saved for her something better than maternity, virginity.

And so that other Virgin, Holy Mother Church, celebrates today the Son of the Virgin. About this the Apostle Paul had something to say in his Second to the Corinthians. "I've readied you for one husband, Christ, and presented you to him as a chaste virgin" (11:2). Why does he say "a chaste virgin"? Isn't chaste virginity a rarity, what with so many of both sexes, young men and women, joined together as fathers and mothers? And what's the big deal about "a chaste virgin" anyway? Except that her Faith, Hope, and Charity hadn't been breached by another.

Perhaps that's why Christ made virginity a reality in the heart of His Church; He'd already safeguarded it in the body of Mary. In human marriage the woman is handed over to the spouse, and with it her virginity. But the Church couldn't be considered a virgin if she hadn't found the Spouse to whom she could be given; that's to say, the Son of the Virgin.

7

SERMO CLXXXIX

Christmas #6

NIGHT AND DAY

The Day who made all day sanctified this
particular day for us, my Brothers and Sisters!

The song for today has already been
sung by the Psalmist.

"Sing to the Lord a new song! Who
should do the singing? All the earth should
sing to the Lord and bless His name! From
day to day we should bless the day He
brought Salvation" (VUL 95:1–2; NRSV 96:1–2).

Who's this Day from shining day if not
the Son of the Father, the Light of the light?
That's the Day who sired the Day who was
born of the Virgin today. The Former Day
has no sunrise, no sunset—I call that day
God the Father.

Just what is day if it isn't light? It's not the light of carnal eyes. Not the light we have in common with cattle. It's the light that lights on Angels. It's the light that our hearts see and by it are sanitized.

Night comes and night goes. In a sense we all live in the dark; our only torch is Scripture. But morning comes, and the Psalmist sings, "I'll contemplate the wonder of your existence" (VUL 5:5; NRSV 5:3).

TRUTH HAS SPRUNG FROM THE EARTH

Therefore, that Day, the Word of God, the Day that lights the Angels, the source of light from which we've traveled, has clothed itself in flesh and was born of the Virgin Mary. It was a marvel of a birth, I must say! She conceives, and yet she remains a virgin. She gives birth, and yet she remains a virgin. Her offspring is created out of her whom He'd already created. He didn't minimize her fecundity, but He didn't compromise her virginity.

Who is this Mary, and where did she come from? From Adam. And whence Adam? From the earth. That's to say, both came from the earth. That's why we sing with the Psalmist, "Truth has sprung from the earth." What kind of benison is this? "Truth has risen from the earth, and Justice has looked down from above" (VUL 84:12; NRSV 85:11).

But why us? Well, the Jews, or so the Apostle wrote to the Romans, "had no knowledge of the Justice of God, but wanted to build their own system of Justice without reference to the Justice of God" (10:3).

Just how can a single human go about being just? Can he do it all by himself?

I'll answer these questions with some questions of my own.

What kind of poor person can buy himself? How can a person who owns no clothes dress up unless the ragman helps him out?

So just where does Justice come from? From Faith. Paul to the Romans again. "The just man lives on faith" (1:17). The person who says he's just but hasn't the faith to prove it, lies. What would prevent a man with no faith from lying anyway? If he wants to speak the Truth, he'll find the way to do it.

Of course, I have to say, "the Truth that has sprung from the earth" has been a long time in the coming. Of course, you were asleep when it came to you. Yes, you were dead asleep, but it somehow roused you. It somehow cut a swath right to your front door, lest you get lost right at the start. Therefore, let's say it again, but with a greater understanding. "Truth has sprung from the earth." Why? Because Christ was born of a virgin. "Heaven has looked down from above." Why? So that Humankind, who'd reveled in Injustice, might just come to its senses and repent through Justice.

COMEDOWN AND COMEUPPANCE

We were mortals. We were weighed down by our sins. Our sufferings we carted after us. From the moment we were born, we've been nagged by misery. No need to consult the School of Prophets on this account. Just put the question to the newborn, and you'll see. Babies cry right from the start.

So this is the comedown God experienced when He came down to earth, and this is the comeuppance the earth experienced when the Day of days did finally arrive. "Truth has sprung from the earth." He created everything and, odd thing, He found Himself moving among the very things He'd already created. He made day, and it was on one of those days that He came to earth. Christ the Lord in eternity, without a birthday in the presence of the Father, has a birthday here on earth.

In the beginning was the Word.

If He hadn't undergone human generation, would we have arrived at divine regeneration? In other words, He was born in order that we might be reborn.

A thought.

Christ was born, we know that now, so why do we dillydally when it's our turn to be reborn? He was born. He didn't need to be reborn. But don't we have a desperate need to be reborn?

For whom was this regeneration necessary if it wasn't the person whose generation suffered the torments of the damned?

What's the conclusion?

We should let mercy enter our hearts.

A mother carried Him in her womb—may we carry Him in our hearts.

The Virgin was made heavy with the Incarnation—may our breasts grow heavy with the faith of Christ.

The Virgin gave birth to the Savior—may our soul bring forth salvation, may it produce praise.

May our bodies not be sterile—may our souls be fertile with God.

CHRIST GENERATED TWICE

Generation of Christ by the Father without a mother and from a mother without a father. Both marvelous! The first, eternal; the second, temporal. Of course, this eternal birth had eternal trappings. So why wonder? He's God. But introduce divinity here—He's God—and the wonder begins to tail off. Praise quickly rises to take its place.

May faith be present so that you can believe what took place. Isn't it enough that God was humbled for your sake? That was God who was made man. Cramped was the outbuilding He was born in; crimped was the blanket He was wrapped in; crumped was the manger He was laid in. Who's not to admire? He who furnished the world could hardly find a stick of furniture in that ramshackle hostelry. He who became our food was laid in the food trough Himself.

Approaching the manger were two animals, and in them two persons. According to Isaiah, "The ox recognized its owner; the ass, its master" (1:3). Don't blush to be the beast of burden. You'll carry Christ, and you won't strain under the weight. You'll amble along the road, and He'll sway on your back.

Let's be His beast, then, and let's take Him to Jerusalem!

With him on our back we'll fairly fly to the Holy City!

He knows the way; not a chance to go wrong!

Let's go through Him!

Let's go to Him!

Today's His birthday!

Let's celebrate it today and every year hereafter.

8

SERMO CXC

Christmas #7

THE SHORTEST DAY

Our Lord Jesus Christ was with His heavenly Father when He was born of an earthly mother. By that time He'd made two choices. First, the virgin from whom He'd be born. Second, the day on which He'd be born.

As for the latter, a large segment of Humankind has the mistaken idea that one day can be better than another. Especially when it comes to such things as replanting a field, starting a vineyard, putting up a building, setting out on a journey, even taking a wife. The way they figure it, there's a good day and a bad day for doing just about everything.

So they win some, they lose some, but, I'm quick to point out, the one day they can't choose is their own birthday. There's only one person who can do that, and He's the Son of God. He can choose, with no fear of error, the very best days for everything, including His own birthday. How? Well, wasn't He in on the creation of all the days, the good and the bad, the shortest and the longest, since before the world began?

One thing is sure. He didn't pick the day of His birth as casually as some people've done, hanging the fates of Humankind on the position of the stars. That's the lunatic way of going about it.

What I mean to say is, the day of His birth was just another dreary day in human history. But what made it into a really cheery one for us, as we now look back, was that the Son of God chose to be born on that particular day and no other.

Another perspective.

His birthday has the mystery of light about it. The Apostle Paul put it well in his to the Romans. "Night has passed, dawn has come. Let's toss off the dark coverings and don the flashy armor. Let's hit the pavement, set out smartly, stride right up the middle of morning as if we owned it!" (13:12–13).

Let's recognize this day for what it is, my dear Brothers and Sisters! Let's pretend we ourselves are the day! Yes, when we were living unfaithfully, we were the night. Indeed the slip-sliding in our faith had made the nights longer and colder till day itself was about to be snuffed. That's how it was on the day Our Lord Jesus Christ was born. The shortest day of the year. The Winter Solstice. From this point onward in human history, the nights grew shorter, the days longer.

Therefore, my dear Brothers and Sisters, let's treat this day with all possible solemnity. Not like those flaky infidels who've let their faith slip to their ankles just because the sun appears to be a god. That's not to say we don't appreciate the sun ourselves. Rather it has something to do with Him who made the sun in the first place.

He was the Word. According to John (1:14), He was made flesh for no other reason than to let the sun shine on Him for our sake and benefit. As a human being Himself, in the light of the sun, yes, but at the same time in majesty over all the sun and indeed the whole universe. Even on this, His birthday, the Son of Man may find the sun His plaything, His pull-toy. He stands above, the Son of God, holding the sun in his hand.

Sad to say, some people've managed to cloud their own minds into thinking that the sun was a god and—ahem—worshiped it accordingly. Shading their eyes, as it were, they may've missed the chance at ever seeing the true Sun of Justice again.

TWO NATIVITIES, A NOVELTY

Therefore, my dear Christians, this is the day we should celebrate!

Not the divine nativity, but the human nativity!

The day on which the Son of God contemporized Himself with us!

Why would He do such an outrageous, unpredictable thing?

So that He could make the invisible visible!

So that we could pass through from the visible to the invisible!

One of the happy characteristics of our faith as Catholics is that the Lord has two birthdays. One divine, where time held no sway. One, human, where the pendulum held sway. Both nativities have that marvelous air about them; the former without a mother, the latter without a father. Incredible? Well, if the divine stumps us, how can we possibly explain the human?

Who can get a handle on this creative advance into novelty? It's without precedent! Truly one of a kind! That a virgin should conceive, carry a child in her womb, remain a virgin even after the birthing process—who'd believe such a thing? It's altogether too incredible to be believed!

Well, divine faith can make some sense out of it even if human reason can't. Who's going to be the first to say that the Word of God, through Whom all things've been created, couldn't do the fleshly thing without a mother? Wouldn't that be like saying that He couldn't make the First Man without a father or a mother? I mean, in His Incarnation did He really want to do away with sex altogether? What a shame, especially after He created both sexes! Or could it be that in His Incarnation He really wanted to do homage to both male and female?

Perhaps an illustration is in order here.

It has to do with the Lapse of the First Man, which of course has resulted in the Collapse of the rest of us since. The Serpent considered making his approach to the First Man, but then he thought better of it. He decided that the First Woman was the way to go. He propositioned her, then suggested she talk it over with her husband. But the First Man couldn't make up his own mind!

Well, if it made sense to her, he thought, then it made sense to him. And it'd give them both some pleasure they hadn't as yet enjoyed. The result? Some sad spiritual history. Does it matter who was the weaker or the stronger, the First Man or the First Woman? The Poisonous One stuck them both and swallowed them whole.

So we just can't slap the mask of tragedy on and parade about the stage as a wretched victim of the First Crime! We just can't blame the woman for our spiritual death! We really can't say that she was damned without possibility of rehabilitation. Why? Because the Lord came to find out who'd died, males and females both. Why? Well, truth to tell, both sexes had died the death in that Sweet Garden.

And there was another reason for His coming the way He did. He wanted to honor both sexes. Male in that He came as a man. Female in that He came as a son. As for the smiles of Jesus Christ overcoming the guiles of the Serpent, He was the perfect Antidote.

What's that mean for us today? Well, neither sex should give the

Creator the finger for that horrible trick He played on them in the Garden. The Nativity of the Lord restored to both sexes the hope of salvation.

THE ASS AND THE INFANT

Therefore, our prayer today is that both sexes be reborn in Him who was born today. And today we should celebrate, not just the fact that Christ the Lord began to be, but the fact that He who was always with the Father was brought forth into the light of day wearing the birthday suit He received from His mother. If anything, He was bringing fecundity to His mother. If nothing else, He wasn't mucking up her virginity in the process.

He's conceived, He's born, He's a beautiful babe, but just who is this infant? To say someone's an infant is to say that, among other things, he can't talk. But in the Lord's case, He's both a No-Word-er and the Word of all words Himself. In the flesh, at this stage in his life on earth, He's keeping to Himself—and this the person who teaches the Angels! As Prince and Shepherd of Shepherds, He's announced to the shepherds. He lies in the food trough where the cattle feed; yes, He's their food as well as ours.

As for that holy trough, there was this prediction through the prophet Isaiah, "The ass knows, his master's crib" (1:3). And so is it any wonder then, as Matthew reported, that Jesus, preparing to enter Jerusalem with cheering crowds in front and behind, chose an ass's foal for the trip (21:1–9).

And so on this holy day, my dear Brothers and Sisters, let's just wedge our way into the crowded scene, between the shepherds and the animals, and pay our respects to Him who lies in the trough.

Let's get our nourishment there alongside the ox and the ass.

And let's carry our Lord and Master, with Him holding the rein, all the way to the heavenly Jerusalem.

To conclude.

Nativity from a human mother wasn't without its frailties.

Nativity from the Divine Father wasn't without its majesties.

But what else would one expect?

In His life on earth temporality had its day.

In His life in Heaven eternity had its Day.

THE TIME TO TRUMPET

Today's the perfect opportunity for that earthly psalm to sweep us up to Heaven's heights.

"Sing to the Lord a new song! Sing to the Lord, every land! Sing to the Lord, and bless His name!" (VUL 95:1–2; NRSV 96:1–2).

Let's pay our respects to the "Day from Day" Who was born on this day.

To the Day-who's-the-Son from the Day-who's-the-Father.

To the God from God.

To the Light from Light.

This is the salvation the Psalmist has sung about.

"My God have mercy on us, and bless us! May You light up our face! May we come to know Your way on earth! May we find Your salvation in all the nations!" (VUL Psalm 66:2–3; NRSV 67:1–2).

The words "on earth" the Psalmist repeated "in all the nations." He did the same with "Your way" and "Your salvation." And Jesus Himself echoed these words in John's Gospel. "I'm the way" (14:6).

Moments ago when the Gospel from Luke was read in the church, we heard that Simeon, that blessed old gent, had received a divine response to his prayer. Something to the effect that he wouldn't taste death until he'd seen the Christ of the Lord.

Well, that day came. The infant Christ was laid in his arms, and the old man recognized the Little One as the Great One. "My eyes have just seen Salvation," he said, handing the baby back and shuffling off the scene. "Now that You've kept your part of the bargain, O Lord, I'll keep mine" (2:26,29–30).

Therefore, let's use a Psalm to trumpet "the Day of Day, His Savior, His Salvation"!

Let's blare "His glory among the nations, and his marvelous works among all the peoples" (VUL 95:3/190:2–3; NRSV 96:2–3).

He plays with a ball in a manger, but the manger contains the orb of the world.

He drinks from His mother's breasts but He's fed by His Father's Angels.

He's got Himself entangled with our mortality, but He drapes us with His own immortality.

He enjoys adoration, and He's tickled by lactation.

He didn't find a decent spot at the hostelry, but He's made a nice nest for Himself in the hearts of all believers.

He made infirmity look strong by making fortitude appear weak.

Therefore, let's look up at, more than we look down upon, His fleshly nativity!

What did He do for us? After all, He raised humility to unheard of heights!

All of which is another way of saying, let's burn with His Charity so that we may enjoy His eternity!

9

SERMO CXCI

Christmas #8

DEMOTIONS AND DEMOLITIONS

The Word of the Father, through whom all temporal things were made, was made into something rather temporal Himself. That's to say, flesh; He made His own birthday in our time. And as humanity was dawning, He wanted to have one special day for this holy event.

Remember now, dear Brothers and Sisters, no day of ours turned without His divine nod. Remember, He Himself with His Father preceded all the divisions of time we've come to know. Remember also, on this day of all days in the tide of time, He emerged from His mother.

Man-made Himself, Himself a maker of man.

Why? To what end?

Suckling breasts will rule the stars.

Bread'll starve, Fountains dry up, Lights be doused.

The Way'll be exhausted from the journey, and Truth'll be accused by false witness.

The Judge of the living and the dead will be judged by a judge who's as good as dead himself, and Justice will be found guilty and condemned by the unjust.

The Teacher will be cut to ribbons with whips, and the grapes will be stuck with thorns.

The Foundation'll be hung from a beam.

All strength'll be stressed. All safety, sapped. All life, drained.

All these indignities He bore up under. All these demotions and demolitions He didn't deserve. So why did He allow them? For no other reason, apparently, than to save those who really weren't worth the saving.

Needless to say, in ridding us of the Taint, He carted off so many tons of evil. Happy to say, in this ugly process He Himself underwent no contamination. That's not to say we were deserving of any good. No, we weren't. But He came through for us anyway and in a big way!

How did this all come about?

Well, before history began, before time was invented, He was the Son of God. In theological terms, that meant that, although He was born of the Father, He wasn't created by the Father. In rather more recent times He thought it worth His while to become the son of man. That meant that He was made in the mother He Himself had made. How could that've happened? Having emerged from her, He could spend some time on earth. As for her existence, of course, without Him she was nothing and nowhere at one and the same time.

PASSING THROUGH BARRIERS

So what the Psalmist sang—"Truth has sprung from the earth" (VUL 84:12; NRSV 85:11)—has come to pass, and in an unusual way. Mary was a virgin before conception, and remained so after birth. Absent the possibility that her maternity could muddy her virginity!

There was a similar incident in Our Lord's life. After His Resurrection it was thought that His body'd been spirited away and all that remained was His spirit. During that uncertain time, Luke recorded a scene in which the Lord visited some friends.

"You don't believe your eyes, is that it?" He asked them. "Then touch Me, give Me a whack, hit Me as hard as you can, and you'll feel nothing but skin and bone" (24:38).

Well, that's what He said. As for the so-called solidity of His young muscular body, He'd entered the room where his friends were gathered without benefit of the door having been opened; at least that was how John told it (20:19).

Now, I ask you, my dear Brothers and Sisters, why couldn't an adult who entered closed doors not exit closed membranes as an infant?

Well, the Heretical Hecklers will have none of this sort of talk. Their sort of infidelity might well be expressed in the words, *If Christ's divine, I'll eat my hat!* Habitual believers, on the other hand, will have no such trouble. Moreover, when faith believes that God was born in the flesh, it has no trouble accepting that Christ has risen.

Appearing in robust good health, He passed through a locked door without knocking it down and presented Himself to His friends on the other side, chatting them up quite nicely, thank you. So what's all this fuss about His emerging as the Spouse from the bridal chamber— that's to say, the virginal womb of His mother—without knocking it up?

REAL AND SYMBOLIC

So the only-begotten Son of God thought it worth His while to link up with a human nature. His plan, His design? He wanted to associate a Church that had no marks against it with Himself as the sinless head. As for the Church being a virgin, the Apostle Paul called her that. She was a gathering, a collection, a vagina of virgins, or so he reasoned; not only just physical virgins, but spiritual virgins also, those with pure hearts and minds. As he wrote in his Second to the Corinthians, "I've lumped you all into one virgin and espoused you to one man, Christ" (9:2).

The Church, therefore, imitated in a way the mother of her Lord. Of course she couldn't be a virgin the way Mary was but, symbolically, she was both mother and virgin. So when Christ made His Church a virgin, He had to redeem it, buy it back from the fornication of Demons. But the redemptive transaction in no way sold off the virginity of His mother at the time of His birth.

And as for you, my dear Sisters in Christ here this morning. . . .

From the Church's virginity, which is still fresh, comes your procreated virginity. It too is still fresh, what with your not wanting to spend it in nuptials here on earth. Instead, you've chosen to be virgins and to joyfully and solemnly celebrate, on this holy day, the Virgin Birth.

He was born of a woman, yes, but no man laid so much as a finger on her in the process. He brought to her what she loved, but He didn't take away from her what she cherished. And to you, dear Sisters here today, He wants you to do the same. What you've had to endure since the time of Eve He wants to cleanse. So why would He violate what you love so much in Mary?

FOLLOWING MARY'S FOOTSTEPS

What else can I say to you, dear Virgins, except to follow in Mary's footsteps. She conceived, yes, but there wasn't a man in the room. She gave birth, yes, but she remained a Virgin. Yes, imitate her as much as you can. Not in fecundity, of course; you can't do that, and still call yourselves Virgins. She alone could do both; you, only one. Even if you wished to have both, you'd have to lose the one to gain the other, and then where would you be?

As I just said, only Mary could have both, giving birth to the Powerful One, the One who opened up the possibility in the first place. It just seemed that a unique sort of birth should happen in this unique sort of way. Yes, He's the fetus of one virgin, but that doesn't mean that He isn't someone special to all of you Virgins here this morning. Of course you couldn't bring Him forth as your own son, but nonetheless you can find Him as a spouse in your heart. And such a spouse! A Spouse you Felicity of Virgins may embrace as a redeemer and needn't fear as a penetrator.

The bodily birth didn't burst the mother's virginity. Rather His spiritual embrace had just the opposite effect; it prevented it from being broken through. Furthermore, don't put yourselves down. Don't think that just because you're Virgins, your wombs are sterile. Pious integrity of the flesh has some meaning. More often than not, it correlates with fecundity of the mind. The Apostle Paul didn't mince words in his First to the Corinthians. "Just don't go sit in a corner and not think about the things of this world, like how to put a smile on your husband's face. Just stand up and face squarely the things that are in God's world; that'll put a grin on your face!" (7:32–34).

All of which is to say, as Virgins you can't have a womb full of the most interesting children, but you can indeed have a soul full of the most amazing virtues.

So much about you Virgins, my dear sisters in Christ.

Finally, for the remainder of this sermon I want to address all of you together, dear Brothers and Sisters in Christ.

The Apostle Paul visualized all the chaste people in the world and addressed them as one universal chaste Virgin whom he then espoused to Christ. And so do I this morning. I put it to you. What you're dazzled by in the flesh of Mary, do in the womb of your own soul.

Let me give you a couple of examples. The person who believes in his or her heart that there's such a thing as Justice conceives Christ in the heart. The person who confesses out loud that there's such a thing as Salvation—that's how Paul put it in his to the Romans (10:10)—gives birth to Christ. It's in situations like these that your fecundity will be bountiful, your virginity vibrant!

10

SERMO CXCII

Christmas #9

UNUSUAL BUT NOT UNBELIEVABLE

"Truth has sprung from the earth"—or so the Psalmist has sung (VUL 84:12; NRSV 85:11)!

"Christ is born of the flesh"—and that's what we'll sing today!

We solemnly rejoice with a solemn liturgy.

We prayerfully recollect the Sempiternal Day.

We hotly desire with the firmest hope the eternal gifts.

We prayerfully presume we're the Sons of God. Why? Because we've received the power to be such.

For your sake the Timeless Cause of time has become a temporal effect Himself.

Because of you, my dear Brothers and

Sisters in Christ, the Founder of the World has made His appearance in the flesh. Because of you the Creator has become a creature.

Some Christmas questions.

Why are you mortals so tickled with mortal things? Why, supposing it were at all possible, do you try to hang on to this fugitive life for dear life? For a long time now a brighter hope has burned on earth; so bright that life in Heaven has been promised to earthlings.

Now I know you find this hard to believe, so I ask you to believe something else first. God was made man so that He could make men into gods. Without losing a slip of what He was, He wanted to become what He'd made. That's to say, He made what He already was. How? By adding human nature to Divine Nature without at the same time losing His Divine Nature in that human nature.

We're amazed at the Virgin Birth. We even try to persuade those who don't have a whiff of belief in them to consider the possibility of this admittedly unusual mode of childbirth. Unusual, yes, but not necessarily unbelievable. In a womb that had been stranger to all seed, new seed entered and rose. That womb, hitherward and thitherward a stranger to carnal embrace, brought forth the son of man without the aid of a human father. What about the integrity of her virginity during all this rumpus? Well, her membrane—if that's what you're thinking of—it wasn't dimpled at the moment of conception nor was it damaged at the moment of birth.

It makes one stop and think, doesn't it, my dear Brothers and Sisters in Christ—all this potency floating about, but more to be wondered at is the Mercy of it all! Of course, God could've been born our way, but why would He? Funny thing, though. In a sense He actually did it our way. But again, why would He want to be the only child of His mother? He was already the Only Begotten Son of the Father.

Theologians have their ways of expressing all this.

He was made in His mother just as He'd made His mother in Him. Sempiternal with His Father, all too temporal with his mother. Made from His mother after His mother had been made, but before all things were made by the Father. His Only Begotten Son excepted, of course. The Father was never without Him. The Son was never without her.

A CAUSE OF JOY TO VIRGINS, WIDOWS, MARRIEDS

My dear Virgins of Christ, it's time you rejoiced, jumped up and down for joy—His mother is one of you!

You, of course, couldn't have given birth to Christ, and still remained one of your happy number. But it's for His sake you chose not to bear children at all. He wasn't born of you, no, but He was born for you. If you remember His word, as no doubt you do, you're all His mothers. Yes, you are, because you do the will of His Father. Matthew has Him saying this. "Yes, I have family. Who says I don't have family? Whoever does the will of My Father is family, brother and sister and mother and all" (12:50).

As for you Widows here present today, you too should swing and sway with joy! He's the sort of person who made virginity blossom and bear fruit. Now He's taken your vows of continence and made them holy too.

As for those of you who're living with your spouses, faithfully if chastely, you too should join the festivities! What you lost in the body you've gained in the heart. Yes, the innocence of the flesh you lost by sharing your bodies, but what you've gained is a sort of virginity. Another species of it, really. A virginal conscience. In the same sense that every Church is a virgin.

Some instances of virginity.

In Mary pious virginity gave birth to Christ. In Anna widowed virginity recognized the baby. In Elizabeth both conjugal chastity and aged fecundity marched arm in arm for Christ.

Yes, at every level faithful members did their jobs, just doing what His grace empowered them to. And why not? Christ is Truth, Peace, and Justice. From that it's only a hop, skip, and jump to this. Conceive Christ as your faith encourages you to do. Bring Him forth in the good works you do. In other words, let your heart do in the law of Christ what the womb of Mary did in the flesh of Christ.

However, if any of you happily present today have trouble relating to the Virgin Birth, don't worry. You're already members of Christ. Mary saw to the birthing of your Head. The Church saw to the birthing of you. Yes, the Church is both mother and virgin; a mother through the mechanics of an extraordinary love; a virgin through the mysteries Faith and Piety.

In point of fact, that's how the Church gives birth to whole populations. And that's how they're the members of the One Who's both body and spouse.

A final comparison between the Virgin Church and the Virgin Mary. The Church is also the mother of unity among many.

TRUTH FROM EARTH, JUSTICE FROM HEAVEN

So, in conclusion, one and all here present this morning, let's celebrate the day of the Lord's birth with chaste minds and holy affections!

As I said at the beginning of this sermon, "Truth has sprung from the earth" (VUL 84:12; NRSV 85:11). That has indeed come to pass, as had the rest of the same verse. He's also ascended to the Father and, "as Justice, He's looked down from Heaven" (VUL 84:12; NRSV 85:11).

Yes, He was born of the flesh; and yes, He's above the rest of us (John 3:31).

This Justice He thought highly enough of to commend to us. His very own words, as recorded by the Evangelist John, promised the Holy Spirit. "He'll convince the world of a number of things. Sin. Justice. Judgment. Why sin? Because the people just didn't believe Him. Why Justice? Because I'm on My way to the Father. No, you won't be seeing me much longer" (16:8–10).

As for Justice, He looked down from Heaven. "His egress is from deepest Heaven. His orbit, to farthest Heaven" (Psalm VUL 18:7; NRSV 19:6).

As for Truth, don't let anyone speak derogatively of truth on the ground that it sprang from the earth. For example, when the Spouse sprang from the bridal chamber as if He were issuing from the vaginal womb where the Word of God was joined in oozy embrace with a human creature in a certain ineffable marriage. No, don't let anyone look down on this birth!

Yes, the birth was surrounded with all sorts of wonderments, and yes, since then all sorts of words and things've been inspired by it. But just don't think that Christ, because He dolled himself up as a man, is really just one of us, sin included.

The Psalmist had something to say on this point (VUL 18:6–7; NRSV 19:5–6). "As a spouse bursting from the bridal chamber, he was flushed full red, like a long-legged giant on a cross-country race." Next verse. "The starting point was deepest Heaven."

Therefore, just what is it you hear, my dear Brothers and Sisters in Christ, when I say the words, "Truth has sprung from the earth"? Well, it was both a comedown and a comeuppance. Truth came down from Heaven, so that Truth might come up from Earth. And the starting point of it all? The Spouse started from the fickleness of the bridal chamber, "Christ started from the fastness of Heaven."

Here's another reason why Christ was born today. It's the shortest day on earth. The Winter Solstice. Every day from now on will grow longer. To raise us up to His level, the One had to come down to our level. To make His point, He chose the shortest day for his birth, so that from that moment on daylight would only increase on the planet.

At this point His position in the yearly calendar exhorts us. But His silence as a tot is deafening. What He's saying in his silence—that's to say, by His example—is that He became one of us, and a poor one at that, in order to give us the greatest help possible!

As Paul said in his Second to the Corinthians, He wanted to teach us how to become rich (8:9)!

As Paul said in his to the Philippians, He impersonated a slave who'd lead us to freedom (2:7)!

As the Psalmist thrummed, He sprang from the earth that we might possess all Heaven!

11

SERMO CXCIII

Christmas #10

CONGRATULATIONS ALL ROUND

"Glory to God in the highest, and on earth peace to men of good will!" (Luke 2:14).

When the Gospel was read this morning, this passage leapt out. It was the lector's voice we heard, yes, but it was the Angelic Voice the Shepherds heard. Joyful voices both! Congratulating, not just the woman whose womb brought forth the child, but also the whole human race for whom the Virgin brought forth the Savior. Truly worth all the applause, don't you think?

After all, remaining unblushed after conceiving and giving birth to the Lord of Heaven and Earth—that deserves the plaudits, not of a mess of midwives canting themselves silly, but of a choir of Angels chanting up the divine.

Needless to say, we weren't the first to break the news to the Shepherds abiding with their flocks. Nonetheless today we celebrate His nativity with His sheep.

Therefore, let's all say—and say it as thumpingly as we can—"Glory to God in the highest, and on earth peace to men of good will!"

These divine words, these praises of the Lord, these Angelic Shouts, let's give them a thorough going-over. Let's meditate on them with Faith, Hope, and Charity.

As we believe, hope, and desire, so we'll be "glory to God in the highest." Our spiritual bodies'll rise from the dead. We'll be raptured, swept up into the clouds where we'll be joining Christ. There's one condition, though. While we're on earth we have to busy ourselves for peace with good will.

Life "in the highest"? That's where the kingdom of the living is. Where the Lord Himself is, there the good times are. Yes, we can dawdle there—no shortage of time there.

Yes, we want the good times in Heaven, but we'd rather devote our energies to the good times on earth. How shall we busy ourselves? The Psalmist had the answer, and I'll paraphrase it here, if I may.

"For starters, lock your mouth up lest some evil steal from your throat! Then stitch your lips together lest your burble turn to bombast! That's to say, say *no* to evil and *yes* to good. After that, be a person of good will. Single out peace and pursue it relentlessly, even recklessly. Why? Because peace on earth is for persons of good will" (VUL 33:13–15; NRSV 34:12–14).

ABUSES AND EXCUSES, MALADIES AND REMEDIES

Humankind has the worst excuses!

Here's a sampling from Paul's to the Romans (7:18,22–25).

"I can will whatever I want whenever I want, yes, but to do good is beyond me."

Here's another one.

"What the law of God has to say about the interior man sounds good. But in your member below you discover another law. It's at war with the law of your mind and eventually overruns you." What to do? Be of good will. Hold your course. Cry out when the pain becomes too great.

Yet another excuse.

"Who'll free a wretch like me from the deadly clutches of my lowly member? The grace of God'll do it through Jesus Christ Our Lord."

Some further analysis from the Apostle Paul in his to the Galatians.

"The flesh lusts for what the spirit hasn't approved, and the spirit returns thrust for thrust" (5:17). Brawl, free-for-all, no-holds-barred, bloody noses everywhere.

Another insight from his to the Ephesians.

"He's our peace, the one who made both spirit and flesh one" (2:14). What to do?

Demand your Good Will come to its senses about its concupiscence.

Don't stop imploring the help of the grace of God through Jesus Christ our Lord.

The outlaw flesh fights all attempts to rein it in, even as it's being taken prisoner.

Let Good Will call for reinforcements.

Don't let Good Will lose faith in her own inner reserves.

Even when her reserves are gone, don't let her give the Enemy the satisfaction of knowing he's won.

Why?

Because the Lord's on His way. He's in steady contact with those who believe in Him. His words in this regard were caught by the Evangelist John. "If you stick with my Word, you'll truly be my disciples. You'll learn the Truth, and the Truth'll set you free" (8:31–32).

Yes, He'll come and, yes, Truth'll free you up "from the body of this death."

So, "Truth," whose nativity we're celebrating this morning, "has sprung from the earth" (VUL Psalm 84:12; NRSV 84:11). Why? That peace may be on earth to men of good will.

A question.

Who's the perfect candidate to will and to carry out what one wills? No one but the Lord? Well, He's the One who'll help us, inspiring us to do what we should. Just know that His mercy has preceded our every step, cutting a swath before us. The result? We who wanted to will but weren't able to are nonetheless called by Him and given the power by Him to do what we thought we couldn't.

Let's to prayer again from the Psalms.

"I've sworn, given my word, and I've decided to keep the judgments of your Justice" (VUL 118:106; NRSV 119:106).

Yes, that's my decision too. You've put the fear of God into me, O Lord, and I've promised obedience.

Another malady, from Paul to the Romans.

"I saw another law holding court in my member, legislating against the law of my mind, even convicting me of doing some good, which has now become a capital offense" (7:23).

The same as seen by the Psalmist.

"Discombobulated, that's what I am, O Lord. Revivify me according to Your Word" (VUL 118:107; NRSV 119:107).

A remedy, again from Paul to the Romans.

"Yes, I can will my way out it, but not without help" (7:18).

A remedy from the Psalmist.

"Please accept the words that have sprung from my mouth, O Lord" (VUL 118:108; NRSV 119:108).

Yes, O Lord, I want peace on earth to men of good will.

On this holy day, then, my dear Brothers and Sisters in Christ, these are the things we should be saying, the things our reading evokes and our piety provokes.

What we don't want to do is surround this celebration of Our Lord's birth of a Virgin with all sorts of silliness.

We began with Good Will. We'll finish with Charity. The words are Paul's, once again to the Romans.

Such love'll "flood our hearts," not that we have any control over it; "it's the Holy Spirit who mans the floodgates" (5:5).

12

SERMO CXCIV

Christmas #11

BODACIOUS AND LAUDACIOUS

My dearly beloved Brothers and Sisters in
Christ!

Here we are at midnight. Candles all
around.

You're my children of light tonight,
adopted tots in the kindergarten of the Lord!

Have I got good news for you this holy eve!

It's from the Psalmist!

"Rejoice in the Lord! Raise bold, laudacious sounds as only the just can do!" (VUL
32:1; NRSV 33:1).

Yes, yes, you already know what I'm
going to say, but hear it anyway with a kind
and open ear!

First off, come to love the things you believe!

Then speak out about the things you love!

Yes, we're celebrating this anniversary day—the night before, really. Yes, you expect a sermon and, yes, you're going to get a sermon!

Christ is born!

God of the Father!

A human being from a human mother!

From the immortality of the Father—from the virginity of a mother!

From the Father without a mother!

From the mother without a father!

From the Father when there was no synchronization—from a mother when there was no insemination!

From the Father comes the Principle of Life—from His mother, the end of death!

From the Father comes the One who regulates every passing day—from his mother comes the One who consecrates this particular day!

Before He came, the Father sent a man named John. This John was born at the Summer Solstice, longest day of the year. Yes, each day of his young life the light of day grew shorter. When Christ was born at the Winter Solstice, however, the days became longer. And funny if that just doesn't prefigure what John the Baptizer was saying in the Gospel of John the Evangelist. "He has to increase, yes, but I have to decrease" (3:30).

The Apostle Paul put it another way in his Second to the Corinthians. "Human life should stop looking at itself in the mirror and start looking at Christ through the window." Why? "Those who are living now shouldn't just live for themselves alone. They should live for Christ. After all, He's the one who died and rose for us" (5:15).

Paul's words in his to the Galatians are helpful here also. "Well, yes, I'm alive, or am I? What little life I have is really Christ living in me" (2:20).

How right the Baptizer was! "He has to become more important, and I, less important."

PRAISE FOR FOOD

All Angels praise Him, and for good reason! He's their Food Eternal, vivifying them with Fodder Divine. He's the Word of God. They can't live without Him, but then again they don't have to. He's eternal, and so are they, happily living the good life with no end in sight.

Yes, Angels know when to praise—when it's the lesser to the greater; from themselves to their betters; God with God—Glory to God in the highest!

This sort of heavenly calibration the Psalmist knew well. "We're just the people He pastures, just the sheep He feeds" (VUL 94:7; NRSV 95:7).

Despite our own record of infirmity, but because of our promise of good will, may we—once the Exiles, now the Reconciles—deserve some small measure of peace.

"Glory to God in the highest, and on earth peace to men of good will!" (Luke 2:14).

Yes, my Brothers and Sisters, it's the Angelic Voice we hear today! A rousing ovation! A feathery fluttering! The Savior came to save us today!

What meaning can all this angelistic activity possibly have for us?

Well, they praise Him without having to be asked; we too should praise Him but because we've been asked.

They're His heavenly messengers; we're His carrier pigeons.

Ambrosia aplenty for them; manna galore for us.

A question arises.

Just what was that heavenly fare? The Evangelist John had the answer.

"In the beginning was the Word, and the Word was with the Father, and God was the Word."

And just what's in our trough tonight that we should crow about? "The Word was made Flesh, and dwelled among us" (1:14).

For Humankind to eat the Bread of Angels, the Creator of Angels baked a loaf, the Loaf of Loaves; that's to say, He was made man.

The Angels praise Him by their very existence; we praise Him by our every credence.

They take pleasure in it; we have to petition for it.

They just have to reach for it; we have to go get it.

They have only to open the door; we have but to knock.

MORE THAN ENOUGH

Who among all the humans would know all the treasures of Wisdom and Knowledge? All we can know is that they're hidden in the wealth of Christ's heavenly folds and concealed in the poverty of His fleshly folds.

This inevitable question and its inscrutable answer remind me of a passage from Paul's Second to the Corinthians.

"He was filthy rich, yes, but to help us out of our Earthly Bind, He came a filthy pauper. Oddly, but happily, this poverty became the instrument He'd use to make us rich" (8:9).

How did this happen? Well, when He came to assume mortality and consume death, He looked like one of us. That's to say, considering all the articles in His heavenly haberdashery, He stood in tatters. No matter, He said; such riches as I have aren't lost forever; they've merely been put in a blind trust. The Psalmist'd know what He was talking about.

"For those who are genuinely afraid of Him, He's put away millions in the bank. However, for those who're converting their fear into hope, the payback has already begun. How sweet it is! (VUL 30:20; NRSV 31:19).

Paul put it this way in his First to the Corinthians.

"We know only part of the story now, and we won't know the rest until He comes again" (13:9).

This is why we have to upgrade our readiness.

Yes, as God He's the equal of the Father, but as man He's the equal only of us poor beggars.

That's why He has to tart us up to look like God.

What with Himself being dolled up as a human being, He's been able to make many of us human beings into children of God.

As a slave Himself He's been able to fatten up the other slaves, turning them into freemen who have as their right to feel comfortable in the presence of God.

John in his First put it this way.

"We're sons of God now, but what'll become of us? We don't quite know yet. The only thing we do know is that when He does come, we'll be just like Him. How'll we know that? At last we'll be able to see Him face to face—and He'll look just like us" (3:2).

Two questions.

What kind of treasures are Wisdom and Knowledge and Wealth if they have no currency in our own world?

What good is a mountain of sweetness if it only cloys and clogs?

To both of these questions John had an answer.

"Just introduce us to the Father—that ought to do it" (14:8).

And isn't there somewhere in the Psalms a verse that speaks to this?

"I will've done enough when Your glory shines full blast" (VUL 16:15; NRSV 17:15).

According to John again, the Son and the Father are tight (10:30). And in another place in the same Gospel. "Face to face with the Son means eyeball to eyeball with the Father" (14:9).

Which brings us back to glory again. As the Psalmist put it, "The Lord of Virtues is the King of Glory (VUL 23:10; NRSV 24:10).

Yes, He turns us round and round until we face Him face to face.

Yes, we'll be saved, as the Psalmist put it (VUL 79:4; NRSV 80:4), and that'll be more than enough for us.

Yes, more than enough.

BEGINNING OF THE STORY

As the time has come for me to round out my remarks, it's time for our hearts to speak.

"Turn toward me! Look at me! Don't turn your face from me!" That was the Psalmist's cry (VUL 26:8–9; NRSV 27:8–9).

He'll respond to our hearts. The Gospel of John assures us of that.

"Loving Me means keeping My commandments. Love Me, and My Father'll love you. I'll love you, and you know how? I'll look you straight in the face" (14:21).

The crowd who saw Him with their own eyes and heard Him with their own ears may not've understood Him, but they knew His heart was in the right place. But there was much that they didn't see or hear or feel was just right, according to Paul in his First to the Corinthians (2:9). All this He promised He'd one day reveal to those who really loved Him.

Today we're celebrating the birthday of the Slave of slaves with all appropriate devotion! But, if I may flash forward, there's more to the story than this. The readings during the rest of the liturgical year will show what's in store for us. What they'll reveal will really cut our spiritual hunger and thirst. While we're waiting for all this to happen, we continue our walk in faith—alas—as often away from Him as toward Him.

Yes, we're hungering and thirsting for Justice, as Matthew would describe us (5:6).

We're burning almost to the point of combustion to see the beauty of God.

We can't even imagine, as the Psalmist himself couldn't contemplate, that He was born of the Father "before the daystar was born, before Lucifer was lit" (VUL 109:3; NRSV 110:3).

So what can we do at this midnight Mass tonight?

Well, we can entertain the thought that He was born of the Virgin in the darkness of the night.

We haven't yet grasped the fact that His name was a commonplace before the sun was created, and as the Psalmist has recorded (VUL 71:17; NRSV 72:17).

Let's recognize that His tabernacular tent was pitched on the sun, again as the Psalmist has recorded (VUL 71:17; NRSV 72:17).

The Evangelist John had no insight on the Son's having a permanent and unique residence with His Father (1:8), and neither do we.

At least the Psalmist has recorded Him as a Spouse bounding from the bridal chamber (VUL 18:6; NRSV 19:5).

No, we're not ready to be invited to our Father's banquet yet.

But at least we won't starve to death tonight.

We have Our Lord Jesus Christ right here in the food trough in front of us.

Eternal Food.

Fodder Divine.

13

SERMO CXCV

Christmas #12

TWO TALL TALES

My dear Brothers and Sisters, the Son of
God and the son of man, Our Lord Jesus
Christ, born of the Father without a mother,
has consecrated this day!

Two nativities. The divine one, invisible;
the human one, visible; both beggar descrip-
tion. Yes, Isaiah predicted it—"Who'll tell
the story of His generation" (53:8)—but
which generation the prophet predicted is
difficult to tell. Was it the one where He
wasn't really born so much as He had co-
eternity with the Father? Was it the one
where He had co-temporality with His
mother? Or was it the one where the One
who always was was always born. . . .

My point here—and I do have a point—

but I seem to have lost it. It'll come back to me in a moment. In the meantime. . . .

More questions.

Who'll tell how the Light was born of Light? Was there one light or two?

How was God born of God and there not be two Gods?

Did the birth take place at all? No time passed. Nothing happened before or after. As for the present, it didn't have a beginning, middle, or end.

Perhaps the reason why Isaiah asked who'd tell the story is that there was no story to tell. And if there were a story, the words that made it up would be whistled down the wind.

The generation from a Virgin—who'll tell that tale?

Was His conception in the flesh made in the usual fleshly way?

Reportedly, no.

Yes, His rise from the flesh teased milk from her breasts, but did the birthing fluster her virginity?

No again.

So who'll tell the tale? Which birthday? The divine or the human?

Tall tales both!

BIRTHING ONE, BIRTHING MANY

Where was I? Oh, yes! Christ, son of a virgin, spouse of a virgin.

Yes, He's the Lord our God. He's the Go-Between of God and a man among men, our Savior who was born of the Father and created His mother. Creation from His mother actually glorified His Father. This birth was unique; from the Father's perspective because there was no feminine parturition; from the mother's point of view in that there was no masculine penetration.

Being the son of Mary, and Spouse of the Church He'd modeled after His own mother—this was, as the Psalmist put it, "a rather extraordinary yet particularly pleasing nativity, certainly far beyond the rest of humanity" (VUL 44:3; NRSV 45:2). He gave His mother to us and kept the virgin for Himself.

To this last point the Apostle made this quip in his Second to the Corinthians. "I trained you up for one husband; that's to say, I'm presenting you as a chaste virgin to Christ" (11:2).

In another place, his to the Galatians, he said much the same thing. "Our mother isn't a slave or a servant. She's a freewoman. With no husbandly help she's had more sons than the woman who has a husband yet breeds children only for slavery (4:26,27).

Therefore, like Mary, the Church has timeless virginity and seedless fecundity. What Mary has merited in the flesh, and what the Church has preserved in her memory, is nothing if it isn't that she gave birth to the One, and the Church gave birth to the many. Which many, much to the consternation of the chief priests and Pharisees, at least according to the Evangelist John, had to be gathered into one through the good offices of the One (11:52).

WHY CHRIST CAME IN THE FLESH

Further to my point, why Christ came in the flesh.

This is the day on which He came into the world, He through whom the world was made in the first place. He was made present in the flesh, He whose powerful presence was never absent from space. As John the Evangelist put it, "He was in the world for all to see, but nobody seemed to notice. The Light shone upon the darkness, and the darkness swallowed it up" (1:10,1:5).

Then He showed up in the flesh, claiming He wanted to cleanse the vices of the flesh. As John described it in his Gospel (9:6), He mixed spit with dirt to form a medicinal compound, which He then applied to all kinds of blindness, interior as well as exterior, spiritual as well as material. Our inner sight restored, we who were darkness were now daylight in the Lord, according to Paul in his to the Ephesians (5:8). It's a special light, shining only when someone's present. Even then, it'll be seen but only by those spelunking for the Truth.

And this was why, as the Psalmist described, "the Bridegroom did cartwheels as He came from the bridal chamber," "happily racing around the track with giant strides" (VUL 18:6; NRSV 19:5).

Handsome as a bridegroom, strong as a Hercules, lovable yet terrible, severe yet serene, reassuring to the good, rough on the wicked. Hithering in the bosom of His Father, yet thithering in the womb of His mother.

"In the bridal chamber"—that's to say, the virginal womb—divine nature became one with human nature. That's where "the Word was made flesh for us; flesh that'd proceed from His mother and dwell among us" (John 1:14). At the same time, preceding time, going to the Father to prepare a place for us.

Therefore, let's celebrate this temporal day with solemnity!

Let's desire that Eternal Day with hilarity!

Both days through Him who lives in spontaneity but was born for us in contemporaneity!

14

⁂

SERMO CXCVI

Christmas #13

TWO BIRTHS

This very day is the birthday of Our Lord
Jesus Christ!

It's a feast day for us!

The Day of days has flooded this day for
us with the Light of His Son!

It's also the Winter Solstice. The shortest
day of the year. From this day forward Daylight—the light of the Day—will grow
longer.

Did I say it was a birthday? I meant to
say it was two birthdays we're celebrating
today. One divine, the other human. Both are
out of this world, I must say! One without a
woman for a mother; the other without a
man as father.

What was it that Isaiah asked? "Who'll

tell of His birth?" (53:8). Was the holy Prophet referring to both births or to just one? Who indeed could do Justice to the story of God doing the generative act? Or a woman doing the virginal birth? The former when there was no such thing as time; the latter on one specific day. Both without human engineering but not without human admiration.

About that first birth.

We find it in John (1:1).

"In the beginning was the Word, and the Word was with God, and God was the Word."

Whose Word?

The Father Himself.

What Word?

The Son Himself.

Never the One without the Other.

The One who was never without the Son sired the Son. He sired Him, yes, but He didn't begin Him. If He's sired without a beginning, then there's no beginning. Yet He's the Son, and yet He was sired.

"But how could He be sired and not have a beginning?" asks the Heretical Hecklers forever among us. "If He was, then He has a beginning. If He wasn't, then how was He sired, since we know He came to be? How? How? How?"

Well, how should I know? I'm only a human being. I don't know how God was begotten. I've labored to find out, I must say. That's why I've appealed to the Prophet. "Who'll tell the story of His birth?"

Now for that other birth, the human birth. Follow me closely, even though I'll fare no better. It's the one in which "He dumped His divinity in favor of the form of a slave." That was how Paul described it to the Philippians (2:7).

Can we wrap our minds around this?

Can we do any better with the previous sentence in the same holy letter?

"When He was in the form of God, He didn't think it a stretch, a reach, to be on a par with God" (2:6).

Who can get to the bottom of all this? Who'll tell the story behind the story? Saying it is one thing, which is what I'm doing before you this morning, my dear Brothers and Sisters, but thinking it is quite another. Who'd send his mind where no mind had ever gone before? And returning from such a journey, whose tongue could describe what it'd seen? Well, certainly not mine.

So let's just drop this consideration for a moment and return to the previous one. Perhaps there are a few things I can say about it. At least I'll try.

"He divested Himself of His divine trappings, then disguised Himself as a slave; that's to say, He dolled himself up as a human being" (Philippians 2:6–7).

Where?

In the Virgin Mary.

The Angel delivered the message. Kindly the Virgin listened to it. Against her better judgment she believed it. The conception took place. Faith in her soul. Christ in her womb. And that's all there was to it.

A virgin conceives—improbable!

A virgin gives birth—impossible!

After the afterbirth she's a virgin still—too incredible to be believed!

What storyteller—the great Isaiah included—could do Justice to a birth like that?

THREE CHASTITIES

Now, my dearly beloved Sisters in Christ, something especially for you.

As the life of the Church began, there were three ways for chaste women to live. A wife, a widow, a virgin. As the life of the Church developed, all three cried out to High Heaven the name of Christ!

First, life as a wife. By the time the Virgin Mary conceived, Elizabeth wife of Zacharias had already conceived, bearing in her womb the herald of this Judge. Wanting to share the joy, Holy Mary went to visit her cousin. The fetus in Elizabeth gave the wall of her womb a good swift kick. The son rejoiced, the mother prophesied. Here you have a good example of conjugal chastity.

Where would we find an example of a widow? How about Anna? Just now when the Gospel was read, you heard about her. A prophetess. One hundred and five years old. Having married at fourteen, she lived seven years with her husband before he up and died. For the next eighty-four she was a regular in the Temple, servicing the hours of the day and night with her prayers.

As for life as a virgin, Mary's the premiere example of that.

Which is the right one for you, my dear Sisters in Christ? Wife, widow, virgin? Pick one, and stick to it. If none of them appeals to you, then you're not one of the members of Christ.

Now I know there are wives here today, and I know what you're going to say. "Don't tell us how to behave toward Christ!" Well, I won't. But I just want to say, holy women can have husbands too.

What of you Virgins today? Chaste, and proud of it! Well, you know what Jesus the son of Sirach had to say about that. "The more they swagger, the more they slither. That's to say, the more they crow about the wonderfulness of themselves, the more they should shush their virtues from the public eye" (VUL Ecclesiasticus 3:20; NRSV Sirach 3:18).

So much for all the examples of Salvation through Chastity that I've paraded before your eyes. The moral? No one should stray from the straight and narrow.

One last observation. If a man wants to take a fling, he should do so, but only with his wife. Better, he not do it at all. Best, he never wive it in the first place!

DOWNSIZING

What a mercy! The Lord Jesus wanted to become man for our sake. Have no fear. Mercy wasn't devalued in the transaction. How do we know? Wisdom lies on the earth.

"In the beginning was the Word, the Word was with God, and the Word was God."

O Bread of Angels! From You they get their fill. Full plates all around. From You also they get their breath, their Wisdom, their happiness. So that's where You are for the Angels.

But where can I find You?

At the back of a roadhouse. Where the animals are housed. Wrapped in a blanket. Laid in a trough. And on whose account?

He nudges the stars, but nurses from the breast.

He fills the Angels, speaks in His Father's bosom, says nothing in His mother's lap.

He'll speak all right, but only when He reaches the right age.

And He'll fill a Gospel for us. He'll suffer on account of us. He'll die because of us. He'll rise from the dead; it'll be a sign of our reward to come. He'll ascend into Heaven right in front of His disciples' eyes. And He'll come back from Heaven for the Judgment.

Look at how He miniaturized Himself so that He could lie in that manger. That doesn't mean He had to leave something behind in order to fit. He just received what He wasn't while remaining what He was.

Behold, we have the infant Christ in front of us.

Let's grow old with Him.

PRESBYTERS AND PERPETRATORS

I think I've said enough to you, my Charity of Christians. So many of you here to celebrate the solemnity!

But there's one more thing I have to say, and it makes me so sad!

The first of January is almost upon us, and you all know what that means. All those pagan, superstitious solemnities at the turning of the year.

Now all of you are Christians, and with God's help this is a Christian city. But there are two kinds of people living here, Christians and Jews. The Jews are God-fearing people with sense enough to avoid the pagan pastimes. But the Christians? Why do the Christians insist on taking part in these frivolities and think they've nothing to lose? In other words, I pray Christians will do nothing to tweak the Divine Pique.

What am I talking about? Iniquity. In all of its forms. Gambling, drinking, dancing, theater-going. But let's not rush to local judgment here. No finger-pointing at which Christian did what un-Christian thing. The Judge of Judges will be coming all too soon. He'll attend to all of that.

So just allow me one moment to remind you that you're Christians. Members of Christ. So ponder this! What a great price Christ has paid for you!

Lastly, a word to the miscreants. Don't turn up your noses if what I'm about to say displeases you. But do you really know what you're doing? You're causing all kinds of sadness and sorrow and embarrassment to the rest of us. Are the Jews doing it? Of course not. That should give you a clue.

I'm thinking now of one specific instance. It took place six months ago, on the feast of John the Baptizer—a suitable time, don't you think, between the birth of the Herald and the birth of the Judge? The Summer Solstice. A few Christians—I mention no names—went down to the sea and splashed about in some sort of ancient pagan purification rite.

Have you forgotten so soon that John the Baptizer had changed all that; that Christian Baptism had changed all that?

I was out of town at the time. When I returned, I heard the sorry news from our Presbyters. They were upset by the sinful way those Christians conducted themselves. Acting in accordance with Church law, they handed out some pretty stiff discipline to the ringleaders.

Of course, as with all Perpetrators, you didn't feel like you'd done a thing wrong. Yes, I've heard your mumbling and grumbling till I'm sick of it.

"It was no big deal, so why are you blowing it up out of all proportion?"

"If only you'd said something about it ahead of time, we wouldn't have done it."

"If only the Presbyters had let out one peep, made just one whisper, we wouldn't have done it."

Well, my dear Perps, if all you needed was a warning, then here's a warning you won't forget!

"Behold the bishop! I'm the bishop here, and I now give you fair warning! My words are meant to advise you, to preach to you, to shake some sense into you!"

And if that isn't warning enough, then how about this?

"This is your bishop ordering you! This is your bishop warning you! This is your bishop asking you! This is your bishop begging you! I call Him who's born today to witness your oath! I extract this oath from you! I bind you with this oath! Don't do it again!"

Well, I've done my duty as bishop. Now you do yours as Christians.

Heed my warning, and I'll spare the lash.

That'll be easier on both of us.

Do heed my warning, though.

You don't want to see me this sad again!

15

SERMO CXL

Christmas #14

FAITH IN CHRIST

What have we just heard in the reading from the Gospel of John, my dear Brothers and Sisters in Christ, is the Lord's voice.

"The person who says he believes in Me—ah well, he doesn't know it yet, but the one he really believes is the One who sent Me" (12:44).

It's a good thing for us to believe in Christ, especially since John had Him saying much the same thing later in this same passage.

"He came into the world as a light" (12:46).

And in another passage in the same Gospel, the Person who believes in Him "won't have to walk in the darkness." Why? "He'll have the Light of Life to walk by" (8:12).

Yes, to believe in Christ is a good thing. A very good thing, indeed. And the opposite is true too. Not to believe in Christ is an evil, a very great evil. Why would I say that? Because Christ, whatever else He may be, is the Son of the Father. Please note that the opposite of this statement isn't true. The Father isn't the Son of the Son—He's the Father of the Son. As such, Christ can recommend faith in Himself while at the same time deferring all honor to the Author of it all.

COMPARES AND CONTRASTS

This is what you have to hold on to, firmly and fixedly, until your grasp grows numb, if you want to survive as Catholics.

Not contraries or contradictories. Just some *compares* and *contrasts*.

In no time at all God the Father sired the Son, and it didn't take Him much longer to make Him in the Virgin and take Him from the Virgin.

The first nativity took place before there was a clock; the second took place by the clock.

Both births were out of this world, so to speak. The one with a mother; the other, without a father. When God gave birth to His Son, He came from His Father, not His mother. When His mother gave birth, she remained a virgin and needed no help from a father.

Having been born of the Father, He can't really be said to have had a beginning. But when He was born of a Mother, we know that today, the birthday of the Lord, was indeed the beginning.

Having been born of the Father, He made us; having been born of a mother, He remade us.

Born of His Father, we were borne into existence; born of His Mother, we were borne from pestilence.

The Father made His Son equal to Himself; whatever the Son has, He owes to His Father.

Whatever the Father has, He doesn't owe it to His Son.

And so we say that God the Father comes from no one; but God the Son comes from Some One; that's to say, His Father.

Furthermore, everything the Son does miraculously, everything He says veraciously, He credits to the One from whom He came. And that's His true identity.

A parallel.

On the one hand, Adam was made a human being; as such, he had some flexibility about what he was and what he could become. He was made just, but if he wanted, he could become quite unjust.

On the other hand, the only Begotten Son of God can't be changed. He can't be converted into something He isn't. Nor can He lose any of His stature. What He was, He has to stay. He's equal to His Father, and there's just not a thing Father and Son can do about it.

Plainly, He who gave everything to His Son when He was born, gave Him all, not because He didn't have it already. Without a doubt, what the Father gave Him was that very equality He already had with His Son.

Just how did the Father do it? Or was He really able to carry it off? Was there a defect in His birth? Was He caught a little short in the beginning, but the Father would help Him catch up a little later? If that's what He did, could the Son be said to have a hole in His pocket, and could He see to its mending at a later date?

I've already said this to you, my Brothers and Sisters in Christ, and never let it go. Grab hold of this notion as if it were your life!

"Everything the Father gave to His son, He gave on His two birthdays, the divine and the human. Nothing added. Nothing subtracted. Nothing missing. Two persons. One God. Equality all round."

TRUE GOD AND LIFE ETERNAL

"The Person who sent Me," the Lord said, and you heard it read here earlier this morning. . . . "The Person who Sent Me, He's the same One who gave Me My Commandment; that's to say, what to say when I arrived. And what's that commandment? Life is eternal" (John 12:49 ff.).

Yes, it's the Gospel of John again. Hold on to it for dear life!

"The Person who sent Me gave Me this commandment. It's Life Everlasting."

Would that He'd give me the strength this morning to say what I need to say to you! I have so little to give, and He, so much, I feel I should rush from the scene in embarrassment, but I won't. "He commanded Me what to say," wrote John. "Life is eternal."

Search the First Letter of John for what he had to say about Christ. "Let's put our belief in that true Son of His, Jesus Christ. He's the true God. He's the Life Eternal" (5:20).

What did John mean by "true God" and "Life Eternal"? Well, the true Son of God, He's the true God and the Life Eternal.

Why did John say, "in that true Son of His"? Because God has many sons, many children. A proper distinction had to be made here by John, and so he added that He was the "true Son of God." Not just by saying that "He's the Son," but by adding, as I've already said, that He's "the True Son." So much for the distinction. For we're all sons, all children, by virtue of grace; but He happens to be the Son of God by divine nature. We've been made by the Father through Him. As for Him, what the Father is, He's made of the same stuff. Can we say the same about ourselves, that what God is, we are also? No? What a shame!

ONLY CHRIST DARED SAY IT

Suppose, just for a moment, that the opposite were true.

Just suppose some ignoramus ups and says, "I and the Father are one" (John 10:30). And suppose he bases his claim, not on the fact that there are family ties here, what with the One being the Father and the other the Son, but on the observation that the Father and the Son always seem to agree on everything.

Well, the Apostle Paul had no trouble saying (and these are his words, not mine) that the Apostles were "one with the Father and the Son." Is this the sort of statement that gives blasphemy a bad name? I don't think so. The oneness the Apostles felt with the Father and the Son had to do with obeying the will of the Father and the Son.

Has the Holy Ignoramus dared say this? If so, then Paul could say the same thing, "I and God are one." And Peter could point out that the Prophet could say, "I and God are one."

But they don't say it. Perish the possibility they'd say it!

They know that human nature's wanting medication, needing illumination, and that's different from divine nature.

No one in his right mind says "God and I are one." Yes, a person can make some spiritual progress; he may achieve some measure of sanctity; he may reach the height of virtue; he may build a stairway to paradise. But never ever is he going to say, "Him and me is tight!"

And there's another reason. A person may be virtuous, but when he trumpets that virtue to the public, he blows it to kingdom come!

ONE BRICK SHORT OF A LOAD?

What else can we conclude in this Christmas rummage?

We just have to believe that the Son is the equal to the Father; that the Son is of the Father; that the Father's not of the Son. The Originator's the Father; the Equalizer's the Son; if He isn't equal, He isn't true.

So what are we saying here?

Well, if He isn't equal, then He's less than equal, less than perfect. But if He's a brick short of a load, then I have some questions to put to that Spiritually Sick Man who'd even entertain such a stupidity. How short is He really? One brick? Two bricks? Three? What? Answer me! And if He can be proven to be short, can He make up for lost ground? If He grows old, will the Father grow old with Him? If the Son's beard grows dark, will the Father's whiskers grow white? And what if there's no growth at all and all the hair falls out? Well, then the Son'll have to remain what He was. One *quadrans* short of an *as*. One *as* short of a *denarius*. One *denarius* short of an *aureus*. That's to say, something short of a perfection, never able to make up the imperfection. In other words, He's less than the Father and, no matter how fast He runs, He'll never be able to catch up.

So you see, that's how you Impious Imps yield up the Son!

That's how you Hairy Heretics blaspheme the Son!

So what's the Catholic Faith have to say about this?

The Son of God is of God the Father. God the Father is not of God the Son. But God the Son is equal to God the Father, born equal, not born less. Not made equal after the fact, but born equal.

Was there ever a time the Father was without a Son?

Of course not!

For one thing, take away the words "was there ever a time" because "there never was a time," at least in eternity. Always the Father. Always the Son. The Father without a beginning in time. Same with the Son. No hierarchy here. And no priorarchy either.

But because God the Son is of God the Father, and the Father is God, but not of God the Son—don't begrudge the honorificence of the Son in the Father. Why? Well, it doesn't just detract a whit from His Divinity.

BELIEF COMES BEFORE UNDERSTANDING

Yes, we come back to the words of John, "I know what He has in mind is Life Eternal."

Bend your ears when I say these words, my Brothers and Sisters in Christ.

"I know that what He has in mind is Eternal Life."

Elsewhere in John, in his First Letter, we read of Christ. "He's true God and Life Eternal" (5:20).

If the Father's commandment is Everlasting Life, and if Christ the Son is Himself Eternal Life, then we must conclude the Father's commandment is the Son Himself. But why can't He be the Father's commandment? After all, He's the Word of the Father.

If you accept the Father's commandment to the Son in the carnal, worldly way we know on earth—as though the Father'd said to the Son, "This is what I want You to do, and are You just going to sit around all day, or are You going to get up and do it?"—are these the sort of words He'd speak to the one unique Word? That's to ask, when He gave the command, did He have to pick and choose His words so that they'd sound persuasive, and not persnickety? I think not.

Therefore, believe and accept, believe and understand, what the Prophet Isaiah said, "You'll never understand if you don't believe first" (7:9).

Can you get a handle on that? Can you open your heart? Listen to the Apostle Paul in his Second to the Corinthians. "Spread your wings! Don't get entangled with unbelievers!" (6:13–14).

But what about those who don't want to believe it before they can understand? Well, they're infidels! And because they see some advantage in remaining infidels, they'll have put themselves beyond understanding. Yes, belief comes before understanding. Not the other way round.

In a nutshell.

The commandment of the Father is Eternal Life. Therefore the commandment of the Father is the Son whose birthday it is today. It's a commandment born, not of time, but of birth.

The Gospel of John puts our mind through its paces, doesn't it? It whittles away the flesh, leaving the spirit alone to comprehend the knowledge of God.

Well, my dear Brothers and Sisters in Christ, that should be enough rummage for one Christmas morning.

If I drone on a moment longer, you'll drift off, never to wake again!

SERMONS

TO THE

PEOPLE

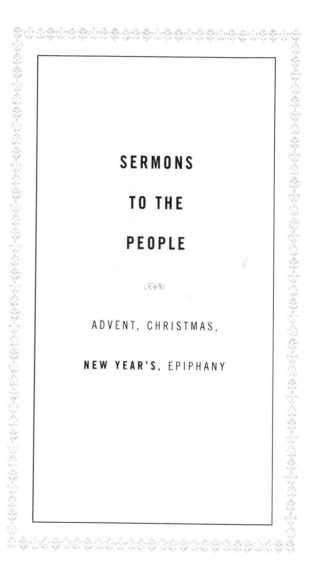

ADVENT, CHRISTMAS,

NEW YEAR'S, EPIPHANY

16

SERMO CXCVII

New Year's #1

AGAINST THE PAGANS

"The wrath of God rains down upon impiety." The quotation is from Paul's to the Romans (1:18).

But whose impiety, whose ungodliness, was he referring to, if not to the Jews' and the Gentiles'?

"But did the Gentiles ever receive the Law?" ask the Heretical Hecklers. "Of course they didn't. So how could they be double-dealers in this regard? Now the Jews are another matter. The anger of God has indeed rained down upon them. Why? The Law was given to them in the first place, but they were unwilling to observe it. To the Gentiles, we repeat, the Law was never given. It's the Jews' fault all the way."

Well, my dear Brothers and Sisters in Christ, it seems Heckle and Jeckle have done it again, forcing us to delve deeper into our own Scriptures!

Let's look again at what Paul said. Let's try to understand how this quotation from Scripture shows that everyone is a defendant in this regard. That's to say, both Jews and Gentiles have a desperate need for salvation and mercy.

Yes, "the wrath of God rains down upon every impiety and every injustice committed by those who detain Truth for some bogus questioning" (1:18).

So much for what the Scripture says, but more important is what it doesn't say. It doesn't say that "they stifle Truth"; merely, "that they've put Truth in protective custody."

"But how can they have Truth now when they didn't have her in the first place?" asks Heckle.

I'd answer with Paul again, from Romans again. "They know who God is and how they should behave" (1:19).

"But how, given the circumstances?" asks Jeckle.

I'd answer again with Paul (1:20). "God the Creator may be invisible, but the things He's created are more than visible to the outer eye; they're seen and understood by the inner eye. His power, for example, and His divinity."

Now, when I say they're visible to the inner eye—that's to say, the intellect—I mean this. Why would a person pay attention to created things, and not to the Creator Himself. For example, you can't help but notice that crops are growing in the fields, fish are leaping from the sea, birds are riding on the breeze, stars are shining in the sky. So why wouldn't it occur to you to cast an investigative eye about for the Creator who did all this?

"Yes, I see them," return Heckle and Jeckle, "but I don't see Him!"

But that's why He gave us eyes, to see created things, I reply. And that's why He gave us minds, to see the Creator of created things. For that matter we don't see our own souls . . . or do we? From the way a body moves and turns and can be made to do things that are difficult, we come to see with our inner eye that there has to be a soul in that body. From there it's only a hop, skip, and jump to the Creator of souls, the One who runs the Chorus Line and keeps them all in line.

But knowing the Creator is only part of the story. At least that's what the Apostle said in his to the Romans.

"Yes, they had a passing acquaintance with God, but they just didn't treat Him as though He was God. Instead, they filled their heads with supercilious thoughts about the here and now, and their foolish hearts clouded their vision" (1:21).

And I'd add to that, "Deservedly so because of their pride."

Read the next verse in Romans. "Their swanning about as philosophers only proved they were fools" (1:22).

They shouldn't claim for themselves what He'd given them in the first place. Nor should they crow about the stuff He gave them as though they'd earned it themselves. Best thing they could do for themselves would be to admit all this. Then they could hold on to what they saw and be cleansed by Him who'd given them the eyes to see it in the first place. If they'd done this before now, then they could've kept their humility intact, been purged, and emerged to take part in the most blessed contemplation. But of course, sad to say, they didn't.

How could this've happened to them? Well, Pride ran riot. The Liar and the Lionizer came knocking at their souls. They had this preposterous selling proposition. A remarkable new cleanser called Pride that removes the stains from their souls. Side-by-side demonstrations were arranged at purification parties with personal friends of the Demons. This was how the Pagans developed their own rites and liturgies, promising that Pride really could work miracles.

As a reward for their pride, they received the anger of God. They should've honored God, but they didn't. Hear the Apostle Paul in the next verse of Romans.

"They dimmed down, dumbed down, the glory of the incorruptible God into a few shabby images" (1:23).

Of course, He was referring to those statuettes of God as man. Specifically, the small hand-held idols so popular with the Greeks and their neighbors. Taking the cake in this regard was Egypt. Egypt had flooded the world with so many flashy figments that the Apostle was forced to enumerate, in addition to "statuettes of God as man," "images of birds, animals, and snakes." Yes, nobody was more superstitious than the Egyptian.

My dear Brothers and Sisters in Christ, haven't you seen in their temples images with the head of a dog or bull or a host of irrational animals? Take a look, a good look, at them. Made in Egypt. All of them.

Yes, the Apostle concluded. "God gave up on them, letting them slide down into the desires of their hearts, there to muck around as they wished, their skin breaking out into ugly little contumelies" (1:24).

These evils of theirs came from their pride. That makes them sins. Not only sins but also punishments. When Paul said, "God gave up on them," he meant that God released them to punishment for the sins they'd already committed.

"Who turned the truth of God into a lie?" Paul asked in his to the Romans (1:25). What did he mean? Well, he was referring to all those people who pushed their cute little images on unsuspecting customers. Of course, these pushers always had an alibi. "It's not the image I worship; the image merely stands for the one I worship." But Paul wasn't fooled by that. "What these people worship are indeed the images themselves; as for what the trinkets mean, they haven't a clue in their heads."

You have to think this matter over carefully. They do indeed worship either the image or the creature. But worship an image like that, and you're turning the truth of God into a lie.

Let me give you another example.

Imagine that the sea is the truth. But Neptune, king of the sea, is a lie made up by humankind. Therefore, Neptune has turned the truth of God into a lie. How? Easy. God made the sea; man, however, made the image of Neptune.

Another instance.

God made the sun; man, however, made the image of the sun; by so doing he turned the truth of God into a lie. "Well, I don't really worship a statuette," they say; "it's really the sun I worship." Don't let them get away with an alibi like that. Paul had it right the first time. "They worshiped the creature rather than the Creator."

CLINGING TO CHRIST

Again, the Heretical Hecklers.

"Christ the Son of God was born with no pretensions, yes, but that was just because He wanted to revel in the nobility of His disciples."

But if that were so, I'd reply, He didn't choose kings or senators or philosophers or orators to follow Him. Instead He chose commoners, paupers, people with no education, fishermen. Peter was a fisherman; Cyprian, a lawyer. Had the faithful fisherman not led the way into the faith, the lawyer with the golden voice wouldn't have followed so humbly. No one should ever despair over his place in society. Rather he should cling to Christ, and Christ'll cling to him. . . .

BUILDING IN CHRIST

Simon wanted one thing in life, to be recognized as a miracle worker and praised to the skies. Pride it was, or so Luke described it in Acts

(8:18), that compelled Simon to think the Gift of the Holy Spirit was for sale. Contrast him with the Apostle Paul who didn't lose his fervor in the noonday sun and, occasionally, gave off flashes of Prudence.

Another example.

As Paul said in his First to the Corinthians, "I've planted, Apollos watered, but it was God who made the crop happen" (3:6). In the next verse he said much the same thing. "The farmer plants and waters, but the crop comes from God" (3:7).

Still another example.

Later in the same passage (13) where the Corinthians confused him with Christ. "Was it Paul who was crucified for you? Were you baptized in the name of Paul?" See how quickly, definitively, Paul refused to be worshiped in place of Christ. He didn't want the fornicating soul to confuse him with the Spouse. Of course, it was a good and proper thing for the farmer to plant and water, but did he amount to a hill of beans? What was Paul afraid of? His life was right. He didn't think his efforts amounted to a hill of beans when it came to the salvation of others. All he wanted to do was build in Christ.

HOPING IN CHRIST

The Apostle Paul didn't want anyone to put their hopes in him, but sometimes that was the price he had to pay as he was spreading the good news about the Lord. Indeed the message he was trumpeting was better than anything he could've cooked up by himself.

In his to the Galatians, he went even further, escalating his point, arguing from the lesser to the greater. "If we, or even an Angel from Heaven, blared anything to you other than what you've already heard, he should be exiled, excoriated, excommunicated!" (1:8).

There was this danger. He saw that a False Mediator could trans-

figure himself into an Angel of Light announcing anything and everything he wanted. Proud men, you know, want to draw all the attention
to themselves rather than to the One and Only God. They want to be
in the center of everything. They want everybody to know their
names. And if it were possible, they'd want to eclipse the glory due
Christ Himself.

A heavenly example of this phenomenon? The Devil and his
Angels.

An earthly example? The Donatists who put their founder Donatus ahead of Christ. That's to say, if they heard a pagan bad-mouthing
Christ, chances are they wouldn't bat an eyelash. But if they heard just
one uncomplimentary word about their dear Donatus, ahhh well!

SPEAKING IN CHRIST

Christ Himself speaks in His saints, wrote the Apostle in his Second to
the Corinthians. "Just what is it you want from me, some sort of proof
that when I speak, Christ speaks with me?" (13:3). But I've already said
that in my First Letter to you. 'The farmer plants and waters, but it's
God who makes the crop' " (3:7).

In all of this Paul's intention wasn't to draw attention to himself.
He merely wanted to bear witness to God. But there it was, as he wrote
to the Galatians, "You welcomed me as though I were an Angel of
God; even as though I were Christ Jesus Himself" (4:14).

In all of His saints, therefore, Christ's held in the highest esteem.
Remember what He said in Matthew? "I was starving, and you gave
Me something to eat" (25:35). Note He didn't write, "You gave the
crowd something to eat." Rather He wrote, "You gave Me." That's
what the Charity of the Head for the rest of its body is like!

ARGUING IN CHRIST

"So what about Juno?" ask Heckle and Jeckle. "She's the Air!"

"You don't give up, do you?" I reply to the Heretical Hecklers. "Earlier on, you insinuated that we worshiped the Sea in the earthern image of Neptune. Now it's the Air. You guys are going to keep running down the Elements until you nail us, is that it?"

"Watch out!" wrote Paul to the Colossians. "There are fallacious philosophers about, juggling the elements of this world until they make your head spin" (2:8). The people he had in mind were the ones who went around justifying idols to those who didn't have the sense they were born with. When Paul wrote "philosophers," he quickly added "juggling the elements of this world." He was sounding the alarum, as it were; warning them to avoid not so much the average idol worshiper as the so-called learned interpreter of idol phenomena.

17

SERMO CXCVIII

New Year's #2

GREETING NEW YEAR'S DAY

We meet again as we'd promised, my dear
Charity of Christians. And I must say, it's
something of a surprise to see so many of
you here this morning. After all, the Kalends
of January hasn't exactly been a solemn occasion in our Church year. Which is another
way of saying, I've never been able to draw
this much of a crowd on such an ordinary
day!

Be that as it may, my dear Brothers and
Sisters in Christ, please don't forget what
you chanted just a few moments ago. After
all, you don't want your tongue to rise to
Heaven while your heart sleeps late. But that
wasn't the case. Both your tongue and your

heart sang out for all to hear. One thing is certainly certain: your singing had God's ears ringing!

As to the words of your chant, and as you well know, they came from the Psalmist. "Save us, O Lord God of Ours; collect us from the nations of the earth so that we may proclaim Your holy name" (VUL 105:47; NRSV 106:47).

Now what's so special about New Year's Day, the Kalends of January? Well, the Gentiles—that's to say, the Pagans and the Disbelievers—have taken it over and tarted it up to a secular solemnity.

Where do they celebrate it? Certainly not in church. Wherever they do it, it's in a secular and sensual environment.

How do they celebrate it? By parading about the streets, carousing at banquets and balls, bawling out mindless chants and soulless anthems. Of course, they could've turned it into a holy day but, Gentiles that they are, all they could do was turn it into a holiday. That's all it means to them.

But what if anything does this truly false feast day mean to us? Not a great deal really, except perhaps this. If you take exception to this extravagant display of Gentile paganism, then you'll be swept away from the Gentiles; that's to say, you'll be gathered up into the Christians. Is that so bad?

CULLING THE CHRISTIANS FROM THE GENTILES

You've certainly chanted up a storm, my dear Brothers and Sisters, and the sound of divine song still reverberates around these holy walls.

"Save us, O Lord God of Ours; collect us from the nations." Those were the Psalmist's words, as I said, lamenting, among other things, the exile of the Israelites. And they're also the text I'm going to

preach from this morning, but with a twist. "Save us, O Lord God of
Ours; collect us Christians from the Gentiles."

So what comes first, the *gathering* or the *saving?* The *saving*, or so it
seems. And from this it follows that the people who mix with the Gentiles can't be called the *Saved*. The *Saved* are those who've been culled
from the Gentiles by the dogged pursuit of Faith, Hope, and Charity.

But before you jump for joy, let me hasten to add that a person has
no guarantee of salvation just because he or she's able to believe, hope,
love. For isn't it true that no one can live this life without these three
affections of the soul? What's more to the point is *Whom* that person
believes, hopes, and loves.

Now here's my point. If you don't believe, hope, love the way the
Gentile Pagans do, then you're no longer one of them. Yes, you do rub
shoulders with them every day, but do remember that in mind and
spirit you and they live in two very different worlds.

How would I describe these two extremes? Well, the Gentile Pagans believe in many false gods, also known as Demons or Daemons
or Daimons, while you, the Gentile Christians, believe in the one true
God. They hope against hope for the half-lives of this world, while
you hope for the eternal life with Christ. They love the artifacts of this
world while you love the Artificer of the world as a whole.

Now, which is the better of the two, the Gentile Pagan or the Gentile Christian? All I'll say at this point is that Faith, Hope, and Charity
can be seen more easily in the lives and deeds of the Christian Believer
than the Pagan Disbeliever.

No doubt, my Beloved Christians, before this New Year's Day
ends, you too will have linked arms with the Gentiles. That's to say,
you'll have tossed, and indeed chased after, all sorts of commemorative
junk like a Pagan. You'll have gambled like a Pagan. You'll have gotten drunk like a Pagan.

Two questions I want to put to you while I have you here in church.

First, how can you, a Gentile Christian, believe, hope, and love like a Pagan?

How can you stand up here and sing, with your lips forming the perfect O, "Save us, O Lord God of Ours; winnow us from the Gentile Pagan Disbelievers"?

Chant that, and if you mean it, there's no doubt that you've distanced yourself from the Gentile Pagans. Of course, you may continue to look like a Gentile, walk like a Gentile, talk like a Gentile, but that doesn't make you a Gentile Pagan Disbeliever.

Second, is there really a distance between Believer and Disbeliever, or am I just making this up? If you really want to know, put it to the test. Just put Faith, Hope, and Charity into practice in your daily life, and you'll see the distance between them and you'll increase with every passing day.

Now let's turn to Our Lord Jesus Christ, the Son of God. He became a human being because of us, and He gave full value for us. That's to say, the ransom was none other than His own life. That having been done, He could then feel free to pick His followers from the Gentiles.

Two observations.

First, the more time you spend with the Gentile Pagans, the less time you'll have to spend with Him, your Lord and Redeemer.

Second, if you live and love, believe and hope the way the Gentiles do, then you're an ingrate, ungrateful to your Redeemer, regarding as worthless the horrific price He paid for you; that's to say, masquerading as the Perfect Lamb, the Perfect Sacrifice.

Two possible courses of actions.

Continue to do what the Gentiles do. Or. . . .

Rearrange your schedule to spend more time following your Redeemer, His blood still damp upon your soul. That's to say, don't continue to commingle with the Gentile Pagans when it comes to the do's and don't's of the moral life.

And for God's sake, don't do anything else they do either! They may toss the colorful New Year's coins, but you should give alms. They may amuse themselves with bawdy ballads from barrooms and barracks, but you should uplift yourselves with scriptural canticles. They may run to the theater, but you should walk to the church. They may binge, but you should fast. And today, if you can't fast, then at least dine in moderation. If you do all these, or indeed any one of these, then you have chanted well those happy words, "Save us, O Lord God of Ours; save us from the fate of the Gentile Pagan Disbelievers."

SEPARATING THE CHRISTIANS FROM THE PAGANS

All that having been said, I can see from your faces that I've caused you nothing but trouble. My words have set your hearts churning. All I said was, Give, yes, but alms to the poor, not those tinny New Year's coins to each other. It's a small thing to give a predetermined amount, but you've got to give more. What's that? You can't afford more? Well then, give at least what you gave the last time.

Does any one of you have a problem with this? Well, don't come up to me and say, *When I spread my holiday coins around, I always get some in return—but when I give to the poor, what do I get? Nothing!* Now that's what the Disbelievers believe. But you don't really believe this, do you?

Well, I must say! If you don't get anything in return when you give to the poor, then you've defected to the Gentile Pagan camp. When you sang "Save us, Lord God of Ours; don't confuse us with the Gentile Pagans," you didn't mean a word of it! Not one single note of it!

How could you have forgotten that old saw from the Book of Proverbs? "The person who gives something to the poor will find that he or she's never out of anything?" (28:26).

Speaking of forgetfulness, I should remind you of those two crucial texts in Matthew. To those who gave to the poor, the Lord said, "Come on in, Blessed of My Father; welcome to the Heavenly Kingdom" (25:34). To those who didn't give to the poor, He'll say, "Trundle them off to the Eternal Bonfire" (25:41).

Now some of you standing here this morning find God's words easy, but others may find them harsh. What can I say? I can only appeal to what's truly Christian in you. If you truly believe, hope, love something that's decidedly, markedly different from the Gentile Pagans, then you have no other choice. You just have to live differently from them. And you'll just have to get used to the fact that your Faith, Hope, and Charity set you off from the unholy customs of those Gentile Pagans.

Give ear to the severe words Paul wrote in his Second to the Corinthians. "Don't yoke yourself with an infidel. Why? That'd be like yoking Justice with Iniquity? Or matching Lightness with Darkness? Or pairing the Faithful with the Unfaithful? And what about the Temple? Can the idols share the same altar as the Lord?" (6:14–16)

And Paul, also known as the Apostle to the Gentiles, said much the same thing in his First to the Corinthians. "When the Gentiles make sacrificial offerings, they offer them up to the Demons, the Devils, but not to God" (10:20). Yes, the Gentiles' religious customs are no doubt a delight to their gods. But as Paul said in the same place, "I just don't want you to become cohorts, companions, co-conspirators, with the Demons!"

What Paul wanted was the separation of those who served the one true God from those who served the many false Demons. Why? Because the Pagans just while away their time singing their ditsy little ditties. They clap their hands at the pompous parades and in the crass theaters. They grab their sides at the insanities of the circus and the cruelties of the amphitheater. And they especially enjoy the intense rivalries of the Pettifoggers who, in behalf of their scruffy clientele from theater and arena, blame every natural pestilence on the rest of Humankind and demand damages in court.

To those very same Demons the gladiatorial participants offer up the dark incense of their wretched hearts. The seducers of the spirit dance for joy on the souls they've seduced.

"But this wasn't the way you learned about Christ," Paul wrote to the Ephesians, and this isn't why you, my dear Brothers and Sisters, sometimes feel attracted to Paganism. "If you'd only heard Christ in person, you would've been inoculated forever against the attacks of the Disbelievers" (4:21–22).

In another place in the same letter, Paul softened somewhat.

"Don't walk hand in hand with the Gentiles. In the past you both were in darkness. Now, because of the Lord, you walk in the light, a child of the Light" (7:8).

We who preach the word of God to you, well, maybe we too can rejoice and enjoy that perpetual light with you.

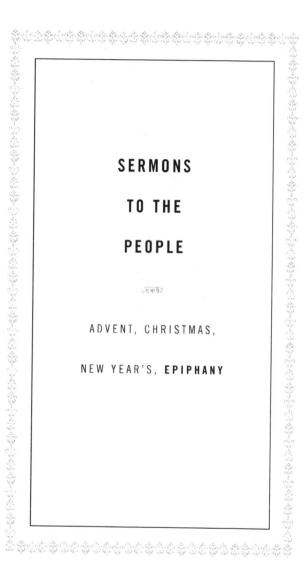

SERMONS

TO THE

PEOPLE

ADVENT, CHRISTMAS,

NEW YEAR'S, **EPIPHANY**

18

SERMO CXCIX

Epiphany #1

CHRIST WASTES NO TIME JOINING
JEWS AND GENTILES

Not so many days ago, my dear Brothers and
Sisters, we celebrated the anniversary of the
day on which the Lord was born of the Jews.

Today we celebrate the day on which He
was welcomed by the Gentiles.

But that was then, and this is now. What
possible meaning can it have for us today?

If anything, it means that "Salvation has
come from the Jews." These are Christ's
very own words, spoken to that Gentile
woman at the well in Samaria; at least as
recorded by the Evangelist John (4:22). Add
to them the words of the Lord, as recorded
by Prophet Isaiah. "Salvation'll reach the

ends of the earth" (49:6). Now that's more than enough meaning for the age we find ourselves living in.

When we celebrated the birth of the Lord two weeks ago, the Shepherds paid their respects; today it's the Magi's turn. Then it was the Angelic Choir who sounded the alarum; today, it's the Wandering Star. Both learned something from Heaven when they saw the King of Heaven here on earth. According to the Evangelist Luke, "there was glory to God in the highest places, and in the lowest places there was peace to men of good will" (2:14). According to Paul in his to the Ephesians, "He was the peace we had, turning both Jews and Gentiles into one" (2:14).

Already, as soon as Christ was born and His appearance as an infant was announced to the world, He was considered to be a rectangular stone; a "foundation stone" or "cornerstone" as the Prophet Isaiah put it (28:16); and this, even as the afterbirth was being toweled from His tiny bum.

Already He began to join to Himself two walls coming at right angles to each other; that's to say, two walls meeting at a corner; the one, the Shepherds from Judea; the other, the Magi from the East.

Already Paul has written to the Ephesians. "He became the joiner, bringing together the two parties into one new human being; two walls into one new domicile; held together by the mortar of peace" (2:15–17).

And so it was at our recent celebration of the Nativity that the Shepherds approached from nearby. But today, at the solemnity of the Epiphany, the Magi have trekked from afar. Two groups of people they certainly were, but there was only one light, the Light of the World— that was what both parties saw. What does it mean? It means that these two holy days must continue to be celebrated by those who come after us.

Epiphany #1

FAITHFULNESS AND FAITHLESSNESS

But what I want to especially talk about today is the party of travelers whom faith led from the remotest places to Christ. That's to say, the Magi, the Scientific Gentlemen who compared what they saw in their skies with what they read in their books. They came to seek Him out. Ever on their lips, at least as the Evangelist Matthew reported it, were questions.

"Where can we find him?"

"Will he really be King of the Jews?"

"Has he just been born?"

"And what about this star we've been following?" (2:2).

The Magi made no secret whom they were looking for. As I said, they asked questions everywhere they went and of everyone they met. And they weren't taken aback by rude replies or no replies at all; they just pressed on with their search.

Does this have any meaning for us?

Well, yes. As we look back today, the Magi seem to point to those of us who have to walk foggily, with faith as our only lamp, desiring to make out what's just ahead; that's to say, hoping to find Christ waiting for us as we round the next bend; that's how Paul put it in his Second to the Corinthians (5:7).

Some questions of our own arise.

As for the Jews, this wasn't a first. Hadn't so many of their kings been born in Judea before this time?

Why was this particular royal tot recognized in the Heavens? And by non-Jews, of all people?

Why did all this happen on the other side of the world?

Why did He shine down from above?

Why did He lie in humility below?

But questions like these only beget more questions.

Who's this new king that's just been born?

Why is He so small?

Why is He so great?

Some answers present themselves.

Christ wanted to give to those very same Magi an unmistakable sign in the sky. He wanted to reveal to their hearts that He was born in Judea. He wanted to open His very own Scriptures to them. He wanted to point to those passages in the Prophets that pointed to Himself coming as a child. And all this because of us. Us He wanted to open the holy leaves.

Back to the Magi. Wandering westward, they eventually came face-to-face with the petty plenipotentiaries of Judea. When they did, they made the appropriate inquiries. Often these officials offered a few Scriptures, but the verses came from their mouths, not from their hearts. Therefore, it didn't take much wisdom on the Magi's part to come to two rather odd conclusions. First, that these locals were infidels; that's to say, they didn't believe in their own Scriptures. Second, that they, the Itinerant Astrologers, were the faithful ones. Happily, by a quirk of grace, the mendacity from the Jewish lips turned to veracity by the time it reached the Magi's ears.

Some moments of greatness.

Great, if the Jewish potentates welcomed this strange news about a new king!

Greater still, if the Jewish princes had them escorted to Bethlehem of Judea, the city they'd pinpointed from the Divine Books!

Greatest of all, if Jews and Gentiles saw with the same eyes, understood with the same mind, and made the same ceremonial visit together to Bethlehem!

After the Jewish tetrarchs and ethnarchs pointed the way for the multicolored Magi to reach the Font of Life, they turned to stone, as it were. That's to say, they became milestones to the Gentiles—something useful to the wheels of the caravan as it passed through—but they became millstones to themselves; they couldn't lift their soles from the ground if their souls depended on it.

Some paradoxes.

The Magi made inquiries with a view to hitting the road and finding the tot; Herod made inquiries, but he wanted to quash the tot.

The Jews were reading where the city in which the birth took place was located, but they had trouble interpreting the time of the coming.

Between the pious love of the Magi and the cruel fear of Herod, there were those who gave directions on the best way to get from Jerusalem to Bethlehem. After they did that, they seemed to fall out of the literature. Later, however, they'd return. They'd deny that Christ was ever seen in Bethlehem; reportedly He'd been born there, but they never did go see for themselves. But if He had been born there, then they would've flayed Him and slayed Him alive. A judicious amount of time would have to pass, of course. Certainly, not while the Holy Tot was learning to gaa-gaa goo-goo. When He did learn to speak that'd be a good enough time.

Alas, that time did indeed come! In a moment of personal terror, aggravated by some really bad advice, Herod let his soldiers loose, and the poor babes, blissful in their innocence and ignorance, met their bloody end.

More paradoxes.

The Magi could suffer for Christ even though they didn't know Him well enough to confess Him for what He truly was.

The Jews didn't pursue the truth of the Teacher of Teachers even though they knew the city of His birth.

SHORTCOMINGS OF ASTROLOGY

That Star in the East—it led the Magi a merry chase, but eventually the Roving Astrologers arrived at the place where the Word of words lay, if not noiseless, then at least speechless. But there, right at that holy spot, a stupidity of stupendous and sacrilegious proportion began to grow.

How can I describe it? An untutored opinion? An unsubstantiated theory? Whatever it was, it began to be bruited about to the effect that Christ was born under some sort of Stellar Decree—and from that grew several bizarre conclusions.

Bad, this star—if indeed it was a star and not some rogue rock hurtling through the air—was seen rising in the East and wandering all over the West.

Worse, some crazies followed it.

Worst, some evangelists swallowed the whole thing whole and wrote it down as gospel.

But the very idea of a Stellar Decree is out of this world! First, it's abhorrent to humans because their entrance into this world is subject to all the terms and conditions of the natural world—but astrology isn't one of them. Second, it's abhorrent to God, that the human Christ should be born under some sort of mystical, galactical determinism!

So what's a person of Christian persuasion to think, let alone to believe?

Well, only Imbeciles chat up the possibility of stars having influence on the genitures of Humankind! Only Harebrains deny they have the will to sin! Only Nitwits cook up excuses to justify their sins! Only the Bellicose blame the Heavens for their disgusting habits; that's why they're so roundly detested by the rest of the population! Only the Pettifoggers circulate what they know to be lies so that they can remain under the supposed patronage of the stars! What I mean to say is,

166

it's only people like these who could possibly think their behavior, their destiny, was regulated by some blinking asteroids.

But if this theory were true, wouldn't it also apply to slaves in a household? So why is it, when these mischievous creatures mess up around the house, the householders beat the living daylights out of them? Shouldn't the stars have foreseen this and taken care of it ahead of time? That's to say, if the householders did believe this theory of Stellar Dominance, wouldn't their own stormy behavior against their slaves be a blasphemy against those nice starry gods who spend so much of their time winking and blinking at the Nincompoops below? Whatever.

Perhaps I oversimplify. But do these Incompetents really think Christ's human birth was the result of a Stellar Decree? Not even according to their craziest conjectures or their most unprophetic and pseudoscientific scriptures! Some ragged wizards seeing a star rising in the East, thinking that some petty king'd been born somewhere over the horizon—that just isn't enough evidence for the Stellar Determinism theory.

From all this some ironies must surely flow.

Christ wasn't so much under the domination of a star as he was Lord of that star. It didn't follow a sidereal path across the sky; rather it made its own surreal, higgledy-piggledy course, leading the Orientals seeking Christ to a particular geographical spot; that's to say, to the place where He was born.

Whence it follows, it wasn't the star that made Christ live a wonderful life on earth, but rather Christ who gave that star such a marvelous appearance. Nor was it the star that decreed the wonders Christ wrought, but rather Christ Himself who demonstrated that the star was just one of the many marvelous coincidences connected with His life.

He was born of a mother, and displayed a new star in the sky.

That's to say, He who was born of the Father who gave form to the Heaven and the Earth, of which the star was just another garish part.

At His birthing a new light was revealed in a star. At His dying an ancient light was dimmed.

At His birthing the dwellers above took on new light, new glory. At His dying the dwellers below trembled with a new fear.

At His rising His disciples caught fire with a new love.

At the moment of His ascending the Heavens learned how to usher Him in with ceremony and courtesy.

So, today, let's celebrate with devout solemnity the day on which, according to the Evangelist Luke (2:8–20) the Shepherds from Judea saw the Christ Child.

Let's celebrate also with equal solemnity this Epiphany day, the day on which, according to the Evangelist Matthew (2:1–11), the Magi from the Gentile lands found Christ and paid their respects.

Christ's the Lord our God, the one who chose the Apostles of Judea as the Shepherds of His flocks. It would be through their efforts, and the efforts of their successors, that He'd gather and save the sinners, not only of the Jews, but also of the Gentiles.

19

SERMO CC

Epiphany #2

EPIPHANY AND MANIFESTATION

From the East the Magi came to pay their respects; that's to say, adore the Virgin's babe.
The anniversary of that holy day we cali-
brate to be today. That's why we celebrate
today. We discharge this duty by a solemn
liturgy and—ahem—a long sermon.

For the Gentlemen Scholars—for that's
what the Magi were—that day was a first for
them. Every year since, it has rolled around
to us, and we greet it with all the festivity it
deserves.

Some ironies.

Those Scholars were the pick, the cream,
of the Gentiles—we're just the full-blown
run-of-the-mill Gentiles.

We read it in the language of the Scriptures, from the mouths of the Apostles—they read it in the stars, in the language of the heavens. The Apostles, the heavens, both told the story of the glory of God (Psalm VUL 18:1; NRSV 19:1). So why don't we acknowledge the Magi and the Apostles? After all, they've become the Seat of God. Doesn't the Book of Wisdom make this sort of leap? "The soul of the Just is the seat of Wisdom" (VUL 9:47; NRSV 8:12,20)?

Throughout these heavens the Architect, Engineer, Builder, and Chief Resident of the heavens let out a roar, a sonic boom. The world shook, then believed. It's a mystery!

At that very moment, He was lying in the manger, tucked away in a stable. He was also leading the Magi from the East. In the heavens everyone knew where He was, but on the earth no one knew where he was. Is it any wonder then that this day is called the Day of Appearance. *Epiphania*, as the Greek language calls it; *Manifestatio*, as the Latin has it.

This day commends both His loftiness and His lowliness. In High Heaven there were sidereal signs for all to see, but it took a mighty trek and a great rummage to find Him in that dilapidated hostel. Invalided as an infant, restricted in a blanket, He was billed and cooed by the Magi. But by the Wicked He was beginning to be a source of fear.

HEROD'S TERROR

Yes, Herod was one of the wicked and, yes, he feared whoever it was. He first heard the news from the Magi who stopped by to ask directions about a mysterious child. What child? he asked. Well, they'd been tracking this star, they said, and they thought the child'd just been born somewhere in the neighborhood.

Well I must say, if a baby bird's nest has the power to make proud kings quake, just what'll the Final Judge at the war crimes trial do to these very same? How much wiser are today's kings, Arcadius in the East and Honorius in the West! They aren't out out-Heroding Herod, seeking whom they can slay! They're more like the original Magi, preferring to pay their respects to Him. Especially when they realized that He was the One who died at the hand of His enemies and indeed for His enemies. He was also the One whose enemies thought they'd killed when in reality He slew death itself.

Still, today's kings should break out into a sweat, but in a pious sort of way, because He's the One who today sits at the right hand of the Father. But in the Magi's day, Herod feared Him though He was only a tot nursing at His mother's teats.

Here's what the Psalmist had to say about a similar situation.

"Kings of the world, you have to come to grips with this. Before you judge the earth, learn the things a judge should know. Serve the Lord with fear. Rejoice with Him, yes, but always sleep with one eye open" (2:10–11).

He's the King, the Avenger of kings who don't have a pious bone in their bodies. But He's also the ruler of the pious kings. He wasn't born the way kings over the ages were. That's because, as the Evangelist John described it, "His wasn't the kingdom of this world" (18:36). That's not to say, the birth was unaccompanied by nobility; there was nobility in the virginity of His mother and in the divinity of the child. Such nobility no Magi ever uncovered in the long line of Jewish kings before Christ. This was the first Jewish king whose birth was marked by a traveling star; the first king the Magi felt they had to come pay their respects to.

THE BLINDED AND THE SIGHTED

There's something that shouldn't go unnoticed here. The farsightedness of the Magi is an eloquent testimony to the nearsightedness of the Jews.

Some ironies.

The Magi were going door-to-door in Judea searching for Him; the Jews had no interest in His whereabouts.

The Magi did indeed find the infant. Yes, He was among the Jews; but the Jews paid no attention to Him then. Nor did they do any better later, when He was walking among them as a teacher.

Here in His homeland these Peregrinators paid their respects to Him when He'd yet to say His first words.

This is the same land in which the citizens would crucify Him as a young man for doing miracles.

The Magi recognized God in the tiny fingers and toes. The Jews didn't spare Him as a grown man doing great deeds.

Could it be that there was more significance in a new star shining at His birth than the old sun weeping at His death?

Furthermore to that same star, the one that led the Magi to the region where the wordless Word was with His virgin mother. It could have led them right to the exact spot, but didn't. Clouds blocked it from their view. Then the Magi had to make inquiries among the Jews as to the whereabouts of the city in which Christ was born or about to be born. The Jews looked to their Scriptures, and found this reference in the writings of the Prophet Micah.

"Bethlehem, land of Juda, you won't be the least among the principalities of Juda. Why? From you will come the prince who'll rule my people Israel" (5:2).

Certainly Divine Providence has spoken here. But what's the meaning behind the meaning? At least this. The Jews'd retain as their own, if nothing else of their Divine Inheritance, only the Divine Scripture. Why this harsh Justice? Alas, they'd closed their eyes to the meaning of Scripture. In it the Jews'd continue to carry the proof of Salvation, but not for them. For us! Yes, these were the very same writings that'd open the eyes of the Gentiles.

Where do the Heretical Hecklers fit in today?

Epiphany #2

Well, every now and then we Christians like to whip out the ancient prophecies about Christ.

Immediately the Hecklers claim that the ancient prophecies aren't all that old.

What we want to know is whether any of those prophecies have actually taken place. And indeed lots of them have.

Instantly, Heckle and Jeckle claim that the reason why so many prophecies've been fulfilled is that they were written after the events prophesied.

Parenthetically, yes, the Hecklers do laugh at us, but we have a rather more serious attitude about them. From among their sorry number we want to rack up conversions. Chief among them, Heckle and Jeckle. End of parenthesis.

The answer to all this, of course, lies in the Holy Books of the Jews. In them are more citations than we need to dissipate the cloud of doubt around the Hecklers' heads. Especially citations about the Pagans themselves, among whom of course we number the Magi themselves. The Jewish Scriptures gave up the information the Magi were looking for; that's to say, the city of Christ's birth. Alas, the Jews themselves made no further inquiries along these lines and, hence, remained in the dark, without the light of the star.

Oh, by the way, after the Magi made their inquiries, the star appeared again and led them on their merry way.

GENTILES AND JEWS, CO-HEIRS

What better time is there, my beloved Brothers and Sisters in Christ, children and heirs of God, to look to your vocation, as Paul called it in his First to the Corinthians (1:26). Cling to Christ as though your love depended on it.

He was manifested to Jews and Gentiles both as a sort of cornerstone.

He appeared in the baby things of his infancy.

The locals saw Him. The foreigners saw Him. The Jewish Shepherds nearby. The Gentile Magi from far off. The Herdsmen on the day of His birth; the Magi on this day; or so we've come to believe.

He made His appearance, yes, but to the Not-so-smart among the Jews and to the Not-so-just among the Gentiles. Yes, there was a shortage of knowledge among the Shepherds, I think we can agree on that, as well as a shortage of religion among the Magi.

As the Cornerstone He joined Himself to both classes just mentioned. Yes, He came, as Paul wrote in his First to the Corinthians, "to pick the foolish things of the world. But why would He do a dumb thing like that? To confound the wiseacres" (1:27). And as Matthew wrote, "to call, not just the just, but the unjust; that's to say, the sinners" (9:13). Why? So that no one might pride himself on his humility, no one might despair of his lack of humility.

Something of the same happened to the Scribes and Pharisees. They'd clouded their own minds into thinking they were the only learned and just people on earth. And in some sense they were. They were more than able to cite and recite the Prophetic Sayings; that's to say, they could've pinpointed the city of birth if they'd wanted to, but they didn't. They rejected out of hand the idea that He was going to become any sort of cornerstone. Wasn't that what the Psalmist had said? The masons rejected the stone, yes, but to no good purpose. "Well, He became the chief cornerstone anyway" (VUL 117:22; NRSV 118:22).

What He promised when He was born, He fulfilled when He suffered and died. So at the one angle of the cornerstone let's cling to Him, cement ourselves to Him. At the other angle are the Jews, "the remnant of Israel saved through the election of grace," as Paul put it in his to the Romans (11:5). The Jews who'd eventually come to join were prefigured by the Shepherds. But we Gentiles were prefigured too, by the Magi who came from afar. As they, so we, nomads no more! We're really citizens with the saints and members of God's family, and want to remain so. We're vertical supports built upon the foundation of the Apostles and Prophets. We're cemented to the Cornerstone, Christ Jesus. As Paul put it to the Ephesians, "He made both into one" (2:14). Why? That we may grow to love unity.

A good example of this oneness would be to collect those poor wild olive branches, once grafted to the one true olive tree, but now stripped off through pride; that's to say, the new Christians who've become heretics. But why would we do that? Well, according to Paul in his to the Romans, "The Gardener will gladly set the grafts again" (11:23).

20

SERMO CCI

Epiphany #3

THE TONGUE OF HEAVEN

It wasn't so long ago, a few days really, that we celebrated the birthday of the Lord. But today's the day He began His manifestation to the Gentiles. Let's celebrate it with no less solemnity. On that far-off day it was the Jewish Shepherds who came to see the Holy Babe. Today it's the Gentlemen from the East who come to pay their respects.

Yes, He was born to be that cornerstone, the Peace of the two walls coming from circumcision and no circumcision, two widely and indeed wildly different angles, that they may be joined in Him who made our Peace and who, as Paul wrote to the Ephesians (2:11–22), "made both one."

Epiphany #3

This was presignified in the Shepherds of the Jews and the Magi of the Gentiles. Fertilization then. Fructification now.

So we have the two days of our Lord—the Nativity and the Epiphany—days that we cherish with spiritual joy. Both felt drawn, the Jewish Shepherds at the Angel's announcing, the Gentile Magi at the star's pointing.

Already the Magi suspected that divinity resided in the stars and took great pains to show their respect to them. But this one star threw all their stargazing and map reading out of whack. How? Well, it revealed the Creator of Heaven and Earth who was worthy of all their respect.

Celestial repercussions? His birth revealed the birth of a new star just as His death obscured the ancient sun. In the light of the one, the faith of the Gentiles was begun; in the darkness of the other, the infidelity of the Jews was brought to the bar.

What kind of star was it? Up to that point it'd never appeared in the skies or on the maps. And from that point it quickly disappeared before it could be identified with certainty and given a name.

That having been said, I'll gladly give that star a name. I hereby name it the magnificent *Tongue of Heaven*. That's a good and proper name because it "told the glory of God," as the Psalmist put it (VUL 18:2; NRSV 19:1). The story that cried out for the telling. The Virgin's Fruit of the Womb and the Wandering Star.

When the star no longer was visible to the naked eye, the Gospel became visible on the horizon and has traveled around the world ever since.

Just what were the questions the Magi asked as they traipsed across the landscape?

"Do you know where He is? The King of the Jews? He's just been born. So where is He?"

Not tough questions really. Already there was a long line of Jewish kings; all of them had to be born. The one the Magi were looking for was just the latest. Surely you know where he is.

Why did the Magi want to meet and pay their respects to the king of a foreign country? According to the Gospel of Matthew, this was their rationale. "We've seen His star in the East, and we've come to pay our respects" (2:2).

How could they've persevered with such great devotion? How could they've kept their desire alive with such tender affection? It had to be that they acknowledged him King of the Jews. And in so doing, they paid their respects to the King of the Ages.

GENTILES EAST AND WEST

Further to this point, Pilate, at least once in his mediocre life, had a whiff of the truth. On seeing Christ in the throes, he wrote down "King of the Jews" (John 19:19). The liarly Jews said that shouldn't be his title at all. "I've written it once," replied Pilate in John, "and I'm not going to write it again" (19:22).

The Psalmist had already prophesied it, if I remember it correctly. "Don't mess with the writing of this title" (VUL ONLY 56:1).

So now let's turn to this marvelous mystery. The Magi were Gentiles, and so was Pilate. They saw the star in the heavens; he wrote the title on wood. In both cases they were seeking and acknowledging, not the king of the Gentiles, but the King of the Jews. As for the Jews, they weren't the ones who followed the star, nor did they consent to the wording of the inscription. Their complete lack of interest would echo down the centuries to the Lord Himself, as Matthew recorded Him.

"The many who've come from the East and West will recline with

Abraham and Isaac and Jacob in the kingdom of Heaven. But the children of the Patriarchs will have to leave their kingdom for the darkness outside" (8:11–12).

The Magi came from the East; Pilate, from the West. They both gave witness to the King of the Jews. To the East when He was born; to the West when He died. The result was that they were invited to recline with the Patriarchs on the soft couches in the kingdom of Heaven. They weren't propagated by the Chosen People; rather they were grafted onto them through faith.

This would be echoed later by the Apostle Paul in his to the Romans. "The wild olive tree has to be grafted onto the one true olive tree" (11:24). For later it wasn't the King of the Gentiles but the King of the Jews that the Magi sought to acknowledge; that's to say, the wild olive came to the true olive, not the other way around. But from the true olive, branches—that's to say, the Jews who couldn't or wouldn't believe—were stripped. That was when the Magi asked where Christ was born, and they answered, at least according to Matthew, "In Bethlehem of Juda" (2:5). Pilate said the Jews were out of order when they requested their king be crucified. Then the Jews became hopping mad and wouldn't stop their howling.

So the Magi paid their respects to the newborn Christ after the Jews identified the place. That was in the Scripture that the Jews accepted and in which we ourselves know Christ.

Pilate, a Gentile himself, splashed his hands as a signal to the Jews who wanted the death of Christ (Matthew 27:24). That's why we wash out the blood stains of our sins in the very blood the Jews have spilled.

As for the sort of testimony Pilate offers by way of his inscription of Christ as King of the Jews, there'll be another time, another place to discuss all this. Passion Week.

JEWS, CUSTODIANS FOR THE GENTILES

Let me say a few final words about the *Manifestatio; Epiphania* the Greeks call it. It began for the Gentiles when the Magi came to pay their respects. And it's interesting to note one more time how, when the Magi asked where Christ was born, the Jews responded, "In Bethlehem of Juda." The Jews knew where, but didn't go to visit Him. Then the Magi left and, following the star, which had now reappeared, they went right to where the infant lay. That's to say, the star could've led the Magi directly to Bethlehem of Juda, but it disappeared behind a cloud until the Jews had answered the Magi's inquiries.

On this point, the Jews were indeed interrogated. They carried the knowledge of their own salvation, but at that one moment in salvation history, they lost it. What they carried now was the knowledge of the Gentiles' salvation. Because of this, that nation was bounced from its kingdom and dispersed around the world; they were a sort of living reproach, a reproof to the faith, but that didn't prevent them from becoming, at least from our point of view, the living proof of the faith.

The temple, the sacrifice, the priesthood, and indeed the kingdom—all of them have been destroyed, but they've managed to keep their name and race intact in a few ancient rituals. Their hope was that these rites'd prevent them from marrying Gentiles, which they felt would be the sure road to extinction. The hope also was that they could somehow retain their slim hold on the testimony of truth. Something like the sign of Cain. No one could kill him, even though he was a proud and envious man who'd just killed his brother (Genesis 4:1–16).

I hope you won't consider this an outrageous reach. The Psalmist wailing to High Heaven for mercy because his enemy has him under house arrest sounds suspiciously like Christ speaking from the persona of His Mystical Body. "My God has proven His power to me. At my signal He'll move against my enemies. But don't kill them, Lord. If you do, my people will forget your Law" (VUL 58:12; NRSV 59:10–11).

How did the prophecies about Christ come down the ages? Through the enemies of the Christian faith. If it had happened through friends, the Gentiles could always think the prophecy passages had been cooked up by the Christians.

Therefore, when the Jews lug in their scrolls, what happens? If I may paraphrase the Psalmist again, God has appeared in our midst once again, but this time accompanied by His enemies. God hasn't killed them off yet. He's left some behind in order to keep His Law alive. These survivors read the Law and observe some of its precepts, and hence keep the memory alive. The results? They only bring judgment down on themselves but, thankfully, they do bear witness to us.

21

✦✦✦

SERMO CCII

Epiphany #4

THE MAN WHO FOLDED HIMSELF

Today, this very day, this very solemnity is
taking place around the world. Yes, it's a
feast day, a festival day, but just what is it
we're celebrating? Just what is it I'm supposed to preach about?

Well, the feast day is called *Epiphania* in
Greek, which in our Latin comes out as *Manifestatio*. Why? This is the day on which the
Magi are reported to have paid their respects
to the Lord. They were piqued by a star appearing in the sky. Not that they knew it at
the time, but the first day they saw it was the
day He was born. Somehow they recognized
it for what it was. And so from that day to
this, they proceeded with all deliberate haste.

When they told Herod their mission,

Epiphany #4

they saw terror in his eyes. When they asked the Jewish scholars to search their Scriptures for prophecies about such a phenomenon, especially where it might've taken place, they were referred to Bethlehem. When they arrived in that city, the star led them to the precise spot—and there He was. They offered him some mementoes of their homelands in the East—gold, incense, myrrh—and were off, but, according to Matthew (2:1–12), by a different route.

That day of the birth the Lord manifested Himself to the Shepherds by way of an Angel from the heavens. That day also, by way of a star in the oriental sky, He was announced to the Magi. That was the day they paid their respects to Him.

Therefore, that day the universal Church of the Gentiles has undertaken to celebrate with extravagant devotion. Why? Well, these Magi—they were just the first fruits of the Gentiles.

Israelite shepherds, Magi Gentiles; so near and so far; they come together at the Cornerstone. Paul put it this way to the Ephesians. "He came to tell the good news about peace to those who were far away and those who were nearby. Yes, He's our peace. He brought the near and the far together and made them one. He folded the two in upon Himself to form one new man whose mission would be peace. He took the two and changed them into one godly body. All of which is to say, He put an end to the animosities between the two groups" (2:11–22).

FIRST HARVEST

The heretical Donatists've never celebrated this day with us, and for good reason. Unity, conformity, uniformity, however one wants to put it, has never been one of their strong points. That's why they've never established relationships with the Church in the East where the star arose in the first place. Yes, it's a feast day for the Gentiles. Let's all join hands to celebrate the manifestation of our Lord and Savior Jesus Christ; for these men were the first harvest of Gentile Christians.

Even before He knew how to call His father or mother by name, the prophecy of Isaiah applied to Him (8:4). That's to say, He received the gifts of the Magi. The strength of Damascus, a banking center where precious metal like gold was king. And the spoils of Samaria, which were the people themselves. Let me explain.

Samaria was a hotbed of idolatry. In fact, the Samarians were able to turn the heads of the people of Israel away from the Lord and toward the idols. But Christ had a different plan. With spiritual sword, He'd go to war against the kingdom of the Devil throughout the entire world. Even as a tot He managed to whisk the spoils of idolatry— the Magi, the Gentiles—away from the domination of idolatry. That's to say, He turned the Magi away from the disease of superstition and toward the adoration of Him.

Odd thing, though. Still not old enough to learn to speak on earth, yet He spoke from Heaven through the star. He showed, not who He was and why He'd come, not with the voice of the flesh but by virtue of the Word made flesh, just who He was, where He'd come from, and why He came.

This was the Word, which in the beginning was God and was with God, just now made into flesh. All that, so that He could take up residence with us and come to us, hithering with the Father while still thithering with us. That's not to say He was deserting the Angels above; rather He was assigning the Angels below to gather men to Himself. He was the Word, yes, but while He was lighting the commute for the Celestial Inhabitants with Incommutable Truth, He was lying in a manger in a broken-down stable. He was the One Who started that star on its course through the heavens. He was the One who started those Magi on their trek to pay their respects.

Yet an infant, and yet so potent, and yet so latent, a Babe who had to flee to Egypt in His parents' arms because of the decidedly hostile acts of Herod. Still unable to put together a string of words, yet speaking to those who'd become His followers by His fact, He said in His silence, at least as recorded by Matthew, "If one city turns unfriendly, then fly to another" (10:23).

Mortal flesh—He was casual about it, modeling it for us, and in it He'd die for us when the right time came. This was why He had to accept the Magi's gifts. Gold, the sign of honor. Incense, the sign of respect. Myrrh, the perfume of death. And, of course, in turn people would die for Him. The Innocent and the Humble. Like the tots that Herod killed. They were the two-year-olds; yes, wrote Matthew, two, the number of precepts on which the whole Law and Prophets depend (22:37–40).

JEWS REVEAL CHRIST

Don't let this observation slip by you.

The Magi inquired as to the whereabouts of the baby Christ. To find the answer, the Jews had to refer to their Scriptures. Yes, they found the answer, but did they do as the Magi did, pay their respects to Him?

Don't we see this even today? Religious practices often harden our hearts. Even while they're revealing Christ for what He truly is, the people don't believe in Him. I'll give you an example. Even while the Jews of today kill the sheep and eat the Paschal meal as the Exodist prescribed (12:9), they're showing off Christ to the Gentiles. Yet it's the Gentiles, not the Jews, who adore Him.

How often have the Doubting Thomases complained that the

prophecies about the Christ to come were cooked up by the Christians themselves? And how often have we had to refer to the codices of the Jews to calm these doubts? Isn't this just another example of the Jews' showcasing the Christ whom the Gentiles adore, but whom the Jews themselves shrug off?

THE LATEST HARVEST

Yes, my dearly beloved Brothers and Sisters in Christ, the Magi were the first harvest of the Gentiles, and we are the latest harvest. We're the inheritance of Christ all the way to the ends of the earth. Yes, blindness crept over the Chosen People, wrote Paul to the Romans, but that allowed us, the Unchosen Gentiles, to become the Chosen People too (11:25).

Once our Lord and Savior Jesus Christ became known, He had to console us, even though He was lying in that decrepit manger. Even now, sitting in Heaven, He feels like He has to sublimate us.

So let's trumpet Him on this earth, in this region of our flesh. Let's not return to where we came from. Let's not repeat every shred, every inkling, of our prior conversations. There's no point in looking back. The Magi didn't return to the Orient by the same route they arrived on. Learn from the past. If you want to change your life, then change your way.

The Heavens've told the story of the glory of God, or so the Psalmist has sung (VUL 18:2; NRSV 19:1). The truth shining from the Gospel, as the star in the sky, has led us to the adoration of Christ. We've perceived with faithful ear the prophecy celebrated by the Jews. It's something of an indictment of them, though, what with their no longer making the pilgrimage with us. We acknowledge and praise

Epiphany #4

Christ the King, Christ the Priest, Christ the Dead-for-us. And we've
honored Him as if with gold, frankincense, and myrrh.
What's left to say, except perhaps this.
Let's not walk the same old path!
Let's strike out and cut a whole new swath!
The Gospel'll tell us how!

22

SERMO CCIII

Epiphany #5

A WORLD-CLASS FESTIVAL

Epiphania is the Greek word, *Manifestatio* is
the Latin word. Whichever you prefer, it was
on this very day that the Redeemer gave all
the nations of the world a second thing to
celebrate. It seems only a few days ago that
we celebrated the first one, His Nativity.
Today we celebrate His Manifestivity.

Therefore, Our Lord Jesus Christ was
born thirteen days ago; that's to say, including both the first and the last day. Yes,
today's the day tradition has it that the Magi
paid their respects to Him.

Two facts.

It has the authority of the Gospel behind it.

And it has, or so it seems, its own authority, what with its having become a worldwide festival. That seems about right, what with the Magi being the first Gentiles to recognize Christ the Lord. They didn't have the Words of Christ to lead them on. Rather they followed the star that appeared to them as a sort of visible speech, an image, as it were, of the wordless Word; as Matthew put it, it was as though Heaven had a tongue (2:1–12). Now the Gentiles gratefully acknowledge that day, the day their first fruits were picked. And we continue to do so, gratefully dedicating this day to Christ the Lord with all appropriate pomp and circumstance.

With regard to Faith and Revelation, the first wave of Jews to encounter Christ were those shaggy Shepherds. On the day of the birth they were nearby and came a-running. They were prompted by the Angels, whereas the Magi were teased by the star. "Glory to God in the highest" is what the Shepherds heard, or so the Evangelist Luke has said (2:14). "The Heavens tell the glory of God," or so the Psalmist has sung (VUL 18:2; NRSV 19:1). Both Shepherds and Magi, the circumcised and the uncircumcised, are like two walls coming from different directions, or so Paul wrote to the Ephesians. Both are laid at angles to the Cornerstone and, cemented there, they rest in peace, making one structure (2:11–22).

GRACE AND HUMILITY

Foreskinnery again. The Circumcised praised God because they'd seen Christ. The Uncircumcised also adored Christ when they saw Him. Perhaps it was that the Jewish Shepherds had prior grace; perhaps the Gentile Magi, more humility.

On the one hand, the Shepherds were minor offenders when it came to sin and hence could respond to Salvation faster and more festively. On the other hand, the Magi, weighing in with lots of sins, required rather more in the way of forgiveness. This, by the way, is the sort of humility the Divine Scriptures make so much of; it's found, or so it seems, more in the Gentiles than the Jews.

Some examples.

From the Gentiles a good example would be that military officer in the Gospel of Matthew. He was very much impressed with the Lord; so much so that he didn't think he could host the Lord in his house. Of course, he could've brought the Lord to his sick servant, but he didn't think it necessary. The Lord's word would do it, as Matthew has reported. That's to say, the Centurion was entertaining in his heart the very Person he wanted, with all due respect, to keep out of his house. Finally, the Lord said, "I haven't found faith like this in all of Israel" (8:5–10).

Another Gentile example would be the Canaanite woman looking for a miracle cure for her daughter. As Matthew recounted it, the Lord called her a dog, and said the children should throw their bread crumbs at her. She wanted to reply to that unfair remark, but she thought better of it. Instead, she played the fool, begging like a dog for the crusts. Hence, she didn't deserve to be treated like a dog, especially since she didn't desire to argue the point with the Lord. Then He spoke to her directly. "Woman, how could I have underestimated your faith!" (15:21–28). What made her humility so great was that she'd made herself so small.

SALVATION OF ALL THE GENTILE NATIONS—FIGURATIVELY LOOKED AT

Yes, the Shepherds from nearby and the Magi from afar both came to pay their respects. This is the sort of humility one finds in the wild olive tree, Paul wrote to the Romans. It makes for a successful grafting onto the one true olive tree a real possibility, with real olives to come (11:17). That's to say, it changed its nature but only through grace.

When the whole world was overrun by the uncut, uncultivated wild olive, its tough wiry fruit became bitter. But when its branches were grafted onto the one true olive, the fruit grew fat and sweet again.

According to Jeremiah they came from the ends of the earth. "Surely our ancestors cultivated lies" (16:19). And they came not just from one part of the earth but, as the Gospel according to Luke said, "from the Orient and the Occident, the North and the South" to recline with Abraham and Isaac and Jacob in the Kingdom of Heaven (13:29).

So the four corners of the earth are called into faith by the grace of the Trinity. Depending on how the calculation is done, four times three equals twelve, the number of the Apostles, a sacred number. That prefigures the salvation of the whole world, coming from its four corners into the grace of the Trinity.

The number twelve has some further significance. It was found on the dish illustrated with different animals. According to Luke in Acts (10:11), Peter saw it, suspended from the Heaven by four lines, raised and lowered three times. Four times three made twelve. Perhaps that had something to do with the Nativity of the Lord plus twelve days making the *Manifestatio*; that's to say, the Magi coming to visit and pay their respects. By this act they merited to receive not only their own salvation but that of all the Gentiles.

Therefore, let's celebrate today with all deliberate devotion.

Let's pay our respects to the Lord Jesus who's resident in Heaven today. The Magi paid their first respects to Him when He was lying in a manger. Then they venerated Him as a sort of once and future phenomenon. Today we venerate Him as a once and completed action.

This first wave of the Gentiles paid their respects to Him when He was sighing for his mother's breasts. Since then the Gentiles, wave after wave, have been paying Him their respects as He sits on the right hand of the Father.

23

SERMO CCIV

Epiphany #6

SUCH A GREAT MYSTERY

A few days ago we celebrated the Birthday of the Lord. Today we celebrate the Epiphany of the Lord. *Epiphania* is a Greek word. In Latin it means *Manifestatio* or *Appearance*.

A good reference point for this appears in Paul's First to Timothy. "No doubt about it, our Christian piety, at least on the hoof, is such a great mystery" (3:16).

And so it's no surprise that both days—Nativity and Epiphany—have something to do with the Manifestation of Christ. Of the first such day He began to be a man when He was born of a human mother; at the same time in Heaven He had no such beginning; just things as usual with His Father. But we on earth can say He was one of us, even though we can't say we've actually spotted Him in His other life.

On that day we call His birthday, a flock of Shepherds from the Jews saw Him. But this very day, which has been tagged *Epiphany* or *Manifestation*, an embassy of Magi from the Gentiles paid their respects to Him. Angels did the announcing in the first instance; in the second, a star did the honors. Angels hung around the Heavens, as it were, with the stars as their pendants. But with both voices over, as the Psalmist might say, the heavens just couldn't keep the glory of God to themselves (18:2).

SO NEAR AND YET SO FAR

To both the Shepherds and the Magi, the Jews and the Gentiles, He was born to be the Cornerstone. This is how the Apostle Paul put it in his to the Ephesians. "He converted Jews and Gentiles into one new human being to the benefit of all. A good beginning, yes, but it'd make it easier for Him at the end when His godly body had to die on the cross" (2:15–16).

Just what is an angle anyway? It's a conjunction of two walls coming from different directions. Where, and indeed when, they touch, can they be said to exchange the Kiss of Peace? Well, figuratively, yes. Up to that point the Circumcised and the Uncircumcised, the Jews and the Gentiles, weren't all that happy. Two walls, yes, but different materials, different shapes. One, the cult of the one true God. The other, the cult of a flock of false gods.

No matter. He took the one nearby and the other far off, and led them both to Himself. "He combined both into a godly body." The Apostle expanded on that. "His dying on the cross was enough to end the hostilities once and for all." Paul went further. "To both the Nomads and the Neighbors He came to preach peace. It was through Him that we both, in one and the same spirit, have access to the Father" (2:16–18).

Doesn't this Scripture passage perfectly describe, demonstrate, prove both walls coming from opposite directions toward the Cornerstone, the Lord Jesus? Yes, they're edging toward Him rather cautiously till they both fit rather nicely. That's to say, some Jews believed in Him, and so did some Gentiles. But it was as though He was beckoning to them both. "Don't be afraid," wrote the Psalmist. "You can approach Him. I think you'll enjoy the results" (33:6).

There's also another Scripture passage. From Peter's First. "I position a cornerstone in Sion. It took some time to find the right one, but for all of that it's a precious stone. Put your faith in Him, and you'll never be tripped up" (2:6).

Well, the Jews and the Gentiles, they both heard and obeyed. Both came, from near and far. They held the peace and put an end to hostilities. They were the first waves, the Shepherds and the Magi. In them, as the Prophet Isaiah described, the animals' perception was heightened. That's to say, the ox could recognize his master, and the ass, the place where his master puts the food (1:3).

A little symbology.

The long-horned animal stands for the Jews; something about the horns and the timbers of the cross that'd be prepared for Christ.

The long-eared animals stand for the Gentiles. Whence that prophetic verse from the Psalms. "Who's served Me well? Well, it's the people I've never met. They heard Me speak, and they did what I asked" (VUL 17:45; NRSV 18:43–44).

Yes, He was Owner of the ox and Lord of the ass and, yes, He was lying in their food trough, a nourishment to them both.

That's how peace came to those who were near and far. The nearbys, the Israelite Shepherds, visited Him on the day He was born, then left utterly delighted. The far-offs, the Magi, took their time about it, experiencing some difficulty, arriving some days after He was born. But when they found Him, they paid their respects and left some gifts.

And so this morning, the Church that has come to be with the Gentiles happily adds the celebration of this day—the day on which Christ was shown to the Gentiles—to the day on which Christ was born of the Jews. And yes, the remembrance of such a great mystery deserves an equal, if separate, solemnity of its own.

WALLS HOLY AND UNHOLY

Let's return to those two walls for a moment, the one from the Jews, the other from the Gentiles, both mortared and morticed, to the Cornerstone. As Paul wrote to the Ephesians, both walls are required by the Spirit so that the bond of peace might hold securely (4:3).

But what about the many Jews who didn't meet the specifications? Shouldn't we feel sorry for them? Well, yes and no. That'd include the movers and shakers described by Matthew in his Gospel (21:21) and Luke in his Acts (4:11). They're the ones who wanted to be doctors, teachers, interpreters of the Law. Well, the Apostle had the last word on them in his First to Timothy. "Quite simply, they were in a fog. That's to say, they had no idea what they were affirming or denying" (1:7).

Yes, they'd clouded their own minds to the point where they rejected the stone, which has since become the Chief Cornerstone, as the Psalmist would put it (VUL 117:22; NRSV 118:22). Of course He wouldn't have that lapidary distinction if He hadn't already offered the two peoples, who had so little in common with each other, a perfect jointure, a pacific juncture, held securely with—ahem—cementing grace.

Don't include in the Israelite wall all the persecutors and executioners of Christ, the ones building up the Law and at the same time tearing down the faith, rejecting the cornerstone and at the same time bringing ruin down upon our wretched city.

And don't for a moment include as part of that Israelite wall the multitude of Jews dispersed throughout the world. They attest to the authenticity of the Divine Writings and tote them about wherever they go, yes, but they don't really come to grips with what's in them. In a sense they're rather like Jacob who had his hip popped from its socket; it was a career-changing event, what with his having to limp from that moment on (Genesis 32:25). And so we may say it was with the Jews after their encounter with Christ.

So much for the Unholy Wall. Now turn your attention to the Holy Wall and include as part of it those Jews who approached the peace of the Cornerstone. That's to say, those in whom Jacob was blessed. Lame, yes, but blessed. Blessed in that some were made holy. Lame in that so many were rejected.

Certainly belonging to that Holy Wall was the lively crowd all around the Savior as He was riding the donkey, the ass's colt, into Jerusalem. The Evangelist Matthew caught the excitement. They raised a chant. "Blessed is He who comes in the name of the Lord!" (21:9).

There's something else to think of in this regard. The Jews who became disciples and apostles. A good example is that Anonymous Christian, referred to in the Greek scripture as *Stephanos,* "Crown"; an appropriate name for one having received the crown of martyrdom; the first after the resurrection of the Lord.

Think also of the persecutors. After the Holy Spirit came, many thousands of them became believers.

And we mustn't forget to think about the Churches. Paul never did, but he did have one regret, expressed in his to the Galatians. "I never had a chance to personally visit the Churches of Judea that were in Christ. A good many of them, though, had heard about me. I was the Grand Persecutor, yes, but now I was preaching the faith in the very same places where I used to pound the living daylights out of them. Such a conversion, they thought! Reason enough to glorify the Lord!" (1:22–24).

That's what the holy wall of the Jews is made of. No wonder it should be joined at the Cornerstone with the wall of the Gentiles!

Yes, it was quite an event when Christ the Lord, the Cornerstone Himself, was laid in the lowly manger, then raised to the roof of Heaven.

No, it wasn't in vain that the Coming of Christ was foretold by the Prophets.

Christ did indeed turn out to be the Cornerstone He was supposed to be.

And what an edifice it turned out to be!

APPENDIX I

HOW DID AUGUSTINE PREACH?

F. VAN DER MEER

Augustine the Bishop: The Life and Work of a Father of the Church, translated by Brian Battershaw & G. R. Lamb. London & New York: Sheed & Ward, 1961. Pages 405–41. *Sine notis.*

How did Augustine preach?

The answer to that question is short and concise. His sermons all have their starting points either in passages in the liturgy, or in extracts chosen by himself from the Bible, and Augustine preached out of, with, and by means of, the Bible.

It is no coincidence that the short homiletic guide which we possess from his hand concerning the general practice of edification by word of mouth should really form the fourth book which he subsequently added on to his earlier work on the correct understanding of Holy Scripture. This work, begun in 397 and concluded in 417, bears the title *Christian Knowledge,* though in our time it would probably have had some such name as *Exegetical Handbook, with a Guide to the*

Biblical Instruction of Christians. It is a book definitely intended for preachers, and its assumption is that whoever ascends the pulpit must have a thorough knowledge of Holy Scripture.

The first three books discuss the value of this most helpful of sciences and explain the rules for interpreting the various meanings of Scripture, particularly its mystical and allegorical meanings. Augustine does not think it necessary to prove or defend the preeminent importance of this last; people in those days were already far too convinced of the greater significance of the mystical and allegorical meaning of Scripture as compared with its literal meaning. The fourth book, which takes up less than thirty folio columns, really does little more than describe the manner in which those giving sermons or addresses should express and deliver what they have found in the Bible.

In many respects this last book is a disappointment. Yet apart from another book that is rather more detailed, namely, his *Instruction for Beginners*, it contains everything that Augustine wrote on the art of preaching and instruction. However, we do not find here any systematic treatise on spiritual eloquence or on the construction of the Christian homily, but only a number of pieces of very excellent advice, all delightfully expressed, combined with a number of examples designed to serve as models. Finally there is a sort of legacy of the old school, namely the division, following Cicero, of the art of speaking into three kinds. Here is a short summary of the contents.

THE BIBLE AND RHETORIC

Augustine begins by saying that he does not intend to restate the rules of rhetoric, though this might be what some readers might be expecting him to do. These rules are no doubt excellent, and most useful to the preacher. Sometimes they may well prove most serviceable

weapons in a debate; but, says Augustine, they are not indispensable—
a very bold observation, even though Quintilian had been dead some
three hundred years.

Indeed, this is another of those occasions on which Augustine,
without willing it, brings about a minor educational revolution. The
rules belonged to the normal school curriculum, and, like Cicero, Augustine thought they should be studied in youth. After that there was
little point in bothering about them, for the preacher has his Bible, and
if he uses it well, the work is already half done.

The right manner can automatically be acquired if one diligently
reads the great authors of the Church—here he refers particularly to
his favorites, Cyprian and Ambrose—and for a time one should also
listen to good speakers. But Augustine places no value on the conscious
study of the speaker's art. Nothing ever really comes of that, particularly when one is no longer young, for an older man speaks quite differently from a young one. In any case, it takes much too much time to
learn all the tricks of the old technique of oratory. With these words
the liveliest speaker of the old school impatiently throws overboard all
the useless antique ballast that cluttered up this subject.

Preaching sometimes means both teaching and explaining, but that
is not really difficult, particularly when one has a public, as one has in
the Church, that is ready to go along with one. To prove something is
sometimes less easy, though it is the kind of thing that always holds
people's attention. But to preach on a theme with which one's hearers
are already acquainted—that means saying something that is already
known, in such a manner that it goes to people's hearts. That is difficult, and is the real test of the artist. A blasé society is liable to be very
demanding, and Augustine himself confesses that he pays more attention to style when in Carthage than when he is preaching in the provin-
cial town of Hippo. In the *cathedra*, however, things are doubly
difficult, for here it is better to speak in a relatively unemotional man-

ner and to depend on the soundness of one's matter than to attempt to move people by empty words.

After these general observations, Augustine deals with the choice of themes and discusses what is their main and largely their exclusive source, namely, Holy Scripture.

THE NECESSITY OF INTERPRETATION

A preacher is nothing but "an interpreter and expounder of Holy Scripture," and his primary aim must be to understand it, to know as much of it as possible by heart and to present it with a certain amount of eloquence.

Holy Scripture indeed already possesses an eloquence of its own— whatever the heathen may say—and how could it be otherwise, for eloquence always goes together with true wisdom. True eloquence has nothing to do with being puffed up, a state which the detractors of eloquence often confuse with the true power of the word: wisdom gives to speech an unmistakable exaltation of style which can be attained in no other way.

Augustine somewhat weakens this moving observation by immediately seeking to substantiate it by a reference to Romans 5:3–6 ("knowing that tribulation worketh patience") and by a further reference to 2 Corinthians 11:16–17, that passionate sequence with the words "That which I speak, I speak not according to God, but as it were in foolishness, in this matter of glorying." He claims that these passages constitute an incomparable *climax* and that they are superb examples of a *periodos*. It is perhaps unfortunate that he had no other terminology but the unduly formalized clichés of Antiquity. He also draws attention to the rich imagery of the Prophets, and analyses Amos 6:16–17 by way of example.

This defense of Holy Scripture may today seem strange to us, but at that time it was supremely necessary that it should be undertaken. Much as today people of taste take exception to the mechanical droning out of prayers, and to the crude sentimentality of some of our images, so in Augustine's day cultured people were repelled by the translations of the Bible into a particularly barbarous kind of Latin. Today the educated unbeliever looks upon the Bible largely as a mythological work but one of tremendous power. In Augustine's day it appeared to him as the possible repository of a certain amount of historic truth, but as something that, from a literary point of view, was not worth serious consideration. The very favor that it enjoyed among the masses may well have increased the educated man's disdain.

There is a celebrated passage in the second book of *Christian Knowledge* in which Augustine tells us that people who had, so to speak, grown up with the Bible, often felt certain correct Latin usages which happened to be unscriptural to be more foreign than the expressions which they had grown used to from Scripture, but which were definitely out of keeping with the classical tradition. Indeed, in Augustine's own case it is obvious from a number of passages that he really admired biblical Latin as a living language and considered it more moving and expressive than the pure but dead Latin of the schools. Many a man of the ancient world must have rubbed his eyes to see whether he read aright as he read such words as these, as indeed must the five Jesuits who, some thousand years later, mutilated our hymns by direction of Pope Urban VIII. Augustine made a better defense of pure poesy than the première of *Hernani*.

After this he speaks of the obscurity of Holy Scripture. It is a thing that must be reverently accepted, but not imitated. God has himself spread this obscurity over it in order to exercise the human spirit and to veil his secrets. However, these obscure passages should only be read to the people when this is absolutely necessary. They are more suitable for study circles or private discussion.

Quite naturally he comes to deal with the question of clarity in interpretation. One should always be as clear as possible, even at the expense of purity of style. What is the point of interpreting at all? Clearly, to make plain the meaning. People must understand us. Else it were better for us to be silent altogether. He reminds his readers of the great freedom which even Cicero had allowed when it was a matter of interpreting texts and tells them to use colloquial expressions whenever the necessity for this arises. If there are two words for the same subject, one correct, the other vulgar but clear, choose the vulgar one. It is even quite permissible, for instance, when speaking of the singular of *ossa* and seeking to distinguish it from that of *ora*, to speak of *ossum* instead of *os*, for if a man is to be edified by anything, the first necessity is for him to understand it. It is not always easy to make oneself understood. I often find it a sad thing, he says elsewhere, that my words do not suffice to express that which is in my heart.

The need for clarity is even greater in a sermon than in discussion, for in church people cannot put questions. It is true that audiences often show by their reactions when they have clearly understood something, and if the signs of this are lacking then what has been said must be repeated, turned about, and restated until the desired reaction is plain to see. Immediately after this, however, a fresh subject should be broached, though that is, of course, impossible for those who "are reciting a sermon that has been prepared word for word and learned by heart." It is no fault if well-known and greatly loved passages of Scripture are frequently brought into the discourse, for one keeps on hearing them read, and whether one hears a thing read or spoken comes to much the same thing, assuming always that the *codex* has been correctly copied. (One must, of course, remember that in those days there were no punctuation marks, and the words were written one running into the other; as against this, people always read aloud even when they were reading to themselves.) The object of all preaching is to unlock meanings, even if when doing so one sometimes has to make do with a wooden key. If the key is of gold, then all the better, but the only thing that matters is that it should fit.

On the other hand, clarity alone, if there are no other ingredients, can become as tiresome as a continual repetition of the same food, however nourishing, and so a certain charm, *suavitas*, is indispensable. Even the prestige of sheer rhetorical ability plays a certain part, and for this reason it is a good thing for a Christian speaker now and then to show people that he can do that sort of thing as well as the next man; and to illustrate his point he quotes a rather pompous passage from Cyprian's letter to Donatus. While doing so, however, he remarks that the saint later abandoned this style. Finally, he says that before preaching one should pray that one's hearers may understand one. One should be a man of prayer first and an orator afterwards.

THE THREE AIMS—EXPLANATION, EDIFICATION, CONVERSION

After thus explaining in a general way how the essential purpose of preaching is to be achieved, he goes on to discuss the technique of the different types of preaching, in this following "a certain orator Cicero."

He distinguishes three kinds, the simple, the flowery, and the pathetic, which are, respectively, designed to instruct, to hold the attention, and to convince; or, to use the language of the Church, to explain, to edify, and to convert.

To these three categories correspond three kinds of delivery, the quiet, the moderate, and the grandiose—*submisse, temperate, granditer*—which in their turn again are the means of instructing, holding the attention, and convincing.

Fundamentally, the material that is dealt with in the *cathedra* is always of the "grandiose" kind, for if God gives grace and we are even preaching over a chalice of cold water, does not a flame, a fire, shoot up out of that cold chalice which can inflame men to works of mercy? One can also say that many things which are discussed in a court of law are of little account, for they are mostly money matters, yet when the standard of Christian perfection is applied, then the least question concerning the fulfillment of duty becomes great.

The matter of justice is like that of roundness; "a large disk is just as round as a small coin," but this does not say that every such matter must be treated *granditer*. That would be unendurable, for nothing wearies men so quickly as the grandiose manner. It is best of all to mingle the three styles (though the *exordium* must always be kept subdued), for each one of them has its advantages and its defects. The interpretative passages should dispense with decorative elaboration, but should glow with clarity of argument.

Exhortations, on the other hand, can really be made more effective by rhetorical elaboration, and here is the true field for verbal brilliance. When an exalted theme comes to be dealt with, then passion will produce its own suitable type of declamation; this will tend to move the hearers and to spur them to action. Applause usually follows a shrewd argument or the elaborated periods of an eloquent exhortation. It is when one speaks *granditer* that the tears begin to flow.

These sayings are rather like flowers from a *herbarium*, yet they do not strike us as faded, for they have recovered in the fresh water of Augustine's own experience. Actually, Augustine gives an example of each of the three styles, taking them from Holy Scripture, from Cyprian and from Ambrose. For the *granditer* he chooses 2 Corinthians 6:2–10, the series of antitheses which closes with the words "as having nothing and possessing all things." Then [for the *temperate*] he chooses Romans 8:28–39, "Who then shall separate us from the love of

Appendix I

Christ?," and [for the *submisse*] Galatians 6:10–20, "I am afraid of you lest perhaps I have labored in vain among you." . . . From each of the Church Fathers he picks a very severe tirade against feminine adornment. At the end he cites Galatians 6:1 and the passage that follows—"Now I say: As long as the heir is a child . . ."—as an example of an emotional passage and of a powerful cumulative effect, but he also uses this passage to show that St. Paul was not expert in the *numerus clausularum*, the harmonious cadences of the different parts of the sentences, and that he did not watch the rhythms of the concluding phrases—matters to which he himself, as he confesses, gave considerable attention.

So he chats away with that easy informality which was the secret of much of the charm of ancient writing, and he tells us that on one occasion he, as it were, visualized all three styles, ranged one behind the other, together with the different effects that each produced. It was, according to his own account, some eight years previously—in 418, that is to say. He had gone, by direction of the Pope, to Caesarea in Mauritania, and had heard from the local bishop that the whole town at a certain time tended to be divided into two camps which did battle with one another in a most desperate fashion. This feud, which had by now become habitual, and was known as "the great row," cost in each year several lives. Augustine was now asked to preach on the matter. At first there was much applause, then the hearers showed close attention, then they were moved to tears, and Augustine was able to say, "Now I've got them where I want them." The feud was ended, and in the eight years which passed between the event and the account of it nothing more occurred.

Among his other observations, he notes that the more entertaining style, by which he means the *moderate* or *temperate* (in which, of course, Augustine the virtuoso came into his own), should not become

207

an end in itself, and that a truth which is all too temptingly presented is liable for that reason to fail to convince certain types of people, though if the matter is handled skillfully a certain gracefulness of presentation is particularly suitable for the work of Christian edification, for it assists internal consent. The circumstance that quiet explanation so often provokes applause is explained by the fact that truth always delights, and when, on top of that, the thing is illuminated by a kind of natural harmony, which is enhanced by the rhythmical speech to which it inspires the speaker, why, then, there is so much applause that the matter can hardly be said to remain at the *submisse* stage.

THE NEED FOR LIVING EXAMPLE

At the end he utters a warning. He leaves all theory aside and becomes the old pastor pure and simple. His last word is this. People are more likely to accept what you preach, if you preach it by your own example. It is truth rather than the word that has a really salutary effect on men. "Christ sent me," says the Apostle, "not in wisdom of speech, lest the cross should be made void." If a man is not a good speaker, then this is no great matter; it is better for him to say wisely what he cannot say eloquently than to say eloquently what he cannot say wisely. If a man simply cannot speak at all, then let the eloquence be in his life. "Eloquent is the man whose life can speak." *(Sit ejus quasi copia dicendi forma vivendi.)*

There is also something that very much concerns his professional colleagues. If a man has a good delivery but lacks an inventive mind, he should not hesitate to appropriate other people's ideas, for there can be no stealing of the word of God, and though Jeremiah says, "I am against the prophets, saith the Lord, who steal my words, everyone from his neighbor," the reference is here to hypocrites; but every man

Appendix I

who ascends the pulpit should first pray, like Esther, "Give, O Lord, a sweet-sounding word into my mouth." He should pray for the people, for himself, for the man who takes the sermon down in shorthand, for all who may later read it, and last but not least, for the author of the book on preaching.

APPENDIX II

※

IN THE MIDST OF HIS
CONGREGATION

PETER BROWN

Augustine of Hippo: A Biography. Berkeley & Los
Angeles: University of California Press, 1969 (1967). Pages
250–58. *Sine notis. Cum permissu.*

Augustine always thought of himself as living among a new "people"—the *populus Dei*,
the "people of God," the direct successors of
a compact and distinctive tribe, the "people
of Israel." It was not for him to inveigh
against Roman society as a whole; it was his
first duty to look after his own, to maintain
the identity and the morale of his "people,"
the Catholic congregation.

Thus, like the old "people of Israel," the
congregation was a mixed body. Differences
in wealth and behavior were only too public
among them. Notably insensitive to infidelity
and fornication, the average Catholic had a
sharp eye for the land grabber, for the usurer
and the drunkard. Like the psalmist in the old
Israel, what moved him was less any modern
"class feeling" directed against the domi-

nance of a group of rich, selfish men in the social life of the town than the galling fact that such notorious sinners had got away with it. "I was angry at sinners, seeing the peace of sinners" (Psalm 73:3).

Augustine had to keep his flock together. It must not be disrupted by envy. He had, therefore, to protect unpopular members rather than exclude them. His deep sense of the compulsive force of habit, for instance, made him more lenient to drunkards than his congregation might have wished. Above all, there is little doubt that his need to preserve the sense of unity in his flock, especially against Donatist criticism, led him to gloss over, even perhaps to collude with, the very real divisions between rich and poor.

Augustine will rarely stand out against the rich in the manner of Ambrose. Ambrose would tell his flock bluntly, that "Naboth's vineyard may be an old story, but it is happening every day." He could inveigh against the local landowners of Milan in the manner of a born patrician, who both knew intimately what it was to be very rich in the Later Empire, and so could despise men who thought of nothing but becoming yet richer. Augustine, by contrast, will often plead for a truce to such unwelcome tensions.

"It is not a matter of income, but of desires. . . . Look at the rich man standing beside you; perhaps he has a lot of money on him, but no avarice in him; while you, who have no money, have a lot of avarice."

"Strive for unity, do not divide the people."

Thus, to feel part of a group mattered far more to Augustine than to denounce his congregation from the outside. He knew that he might follow the example of S. Cyprian in taking advantage of a time of public calamity to denounce the sins of his congregation. Yet, when such a time of calamity came with the sack of Rome, he will prefer to join in with his hearers, addressing them as "fellow-citizens of Jerusalem," talking to them, not of the punishment they would deserve at the Last Judgment, but of their future life, all together, in "that sweet City."

This is the secret of Augustine's enormous power as a preacher. He will make it his first concern to place himself in the midst of his congregation, to appeal to their feelings for him, to react with immense sensitivity to their emotions and so, as the sermon progressed, to sweep them up into his own way of feeling. He could identify himself sufficiently with his congregation to provoke them to identify themselves completely with himself.

Augustine would not even have been physically isolated from his audience, as a modern preacher would be, who stands in a pulpit above a seated congregation. The congregation of Hippo stood throughout the sermon, while Augustine usually sat back in his *cathedra*. The first row, therefore, would have met their bishop roughly at eye level, at only some 5 yards' distance. Augustine would have spoken directly to them, quite extempore; the natural flow of vivid, pure Latin would occasionally lapse, with charming self-consciousness, into an unclassical term, or it would run into a jingle of rhymed phrases and puns, to delight the ear of an illiterate audience.

But there could be little room in Augustine's approach for the relaxed mood of the contemplative. An audience will identify itself only with an excited man; and Augustine would be excited for them; vehement yearnings for peace, fear, and guilt—these are the emotions to which Augustine's audience reacted with shouts and groans. This could be dangerous. When Augustine preached against Pelagianism, for instance, we can see only too clearly how Pelagius, the austere upholder of the autonomy of the conscious mind, was outflanked by a man who could put himself in touch with the more sinister currents of feeling in a large crowd, with their pervasive sexual guilt, and with their terror at the unsearchable ways of God.

Sermons such as these, however, were usually exceptional performances before the excited crowds at Carthage. Augustine was certain of his basic role. It was not to stir up emotion: it was to distribute food. The Scriptural idea of "breaking bread," of "feeding the multitude," by expounding the Bible, an idea already rich with complex associations, is central to Augustine's view of himself as a preacher. The little boy who had once supplied his "gang" with stolen tit-bits, would find himself, as a bishop, still constantly giving.

"I go to feed so that I can give you to eat. I am the servant, the bringer of food, not the master of the house. I lay out before you that from which I also draw my life."

As he told Jerome, he could never be a "disinterested" biblical scholar. "If I do gain any stock of knowledge (in the Scriptures), I pay it out immediately to the people of God."

For Augustine and his hearers, the Bible was literally the "word" of God. It was regarded as a single communication, a single message in an intricate code, and not as an exceedingly heterogeneous collection of separate books. Above all, it was a communication that was intrinsically so far above the pitch of human minds that, to be made available to our senses at all, this "Word" had to be communicated by means of an intricate game of "signs" (very much as a modern therapist makes contact with the inner world of a child in terms of significant patterns emerging in play with sand, water, and bricks).

"Wisdom's way of teaching chooses to hint at how divine things should be thought of by certain images and analogies available to the senses."

And so, by this method, the most bizarre incidents of the Old Testament could be taken as "signs," communicating in an allusive manner, something that would be made explicit in the New.

Once it is thought possible for something larger than our conscious awareness to be capable of active communication, whether this be the "whole" personality, conscious and unconscious of the modern psychoanalyst, or the ineffable "Word" of the Early Christian exegete, an attitude similar to that of Augustine occurs quite naturally. For this communication is regarded as betraying itself by "signs"—by the imagery of dreams, by bizarre remarks, by slips of the tongue; in fact, by *absurdities*, which served as warnings to the exegete and to Freud alike of the existence of hidden, complex depths.

The exegete, therefore, faced with the Bible conceived of as a communication of this kind, will train himself to listen for the single, hidden "will" that had expressed itself in the deliberate selection of every word of the text: for in a sacred text, "everything was said exactly as it needed to be said." Thus the first question he must ask is not "what," "what was the exact nature of this particular religious practice in the ancient Near East?" but *"why"*—"why does this incident, this word and no other, occur at just this moment in the interminable monologue of God; and so, what aspect of His deeper message does it communicate? Like the child who asked the basic question: "Mummy, *why* is a cow?" Augustine will run through the text of the Bible in such a way that every sermon is punctuated by *"Quare . . . quare . . . quare?"* "Why . . . why . . . why?"

We shall see that Augustine's attitude to allegory summed up a whole attitude to knowledge. But his hearers might have had less sophisticated reasons for enjoying the sermons of their bishop. For, seen in this light, the Bible became a gigantic puzzle—like a vast inscription in unknown characters. It had all the elemental appeal of the riddle . . . that most primitive form of triumph over the unknown which consists in finding the familiar hidden beneath an alien guise.

The African, particularly, had a baroque love of subtlety. They had always loved playing with words; they excelled in writing elaborate acrostics. *Hilaritas*—a mixture of intellectual excitement and sheer aesthetic pleasure at a notable display of wit—was an emotion they greatly appreciated. Augustine would give them just this. He could hold them spellbound while he explained why there were thirteen

Apostles and only twelve thrones on which they would sit. Augustine was able to communicate to a congregation his contemplative ascent to God. He could reduce the inhabitants of a whole town to tears. But he would have owed his position as a "star" preacher to the quite characteristic way in which he would settle back in his chair and, like the inspired teacher that he had always been, get his listeners to identify themselves with his own excitement at unraveling a difficult text.

"Let me try to winkle out the hidden secrets of this Psalm we have just sung; and chip a sermon out of them, to satisfy your ears and minds."

"I confess, this is a problem. *Knock and it shall be opened to you.* Knock, by concentrating hard. Knock by showing a keen interest. Knock even for me, by praying for me, that I should extract something from it worth while telling you."

In the unself-conscious routine of these sermons we can come as close as is possible to the foundations of Augustine's qualities as a thinker. Seen in action at such close range, the cumulative impression is quite overwhelming. He is very much the product of a culture that admired a complete mastery of texts combined with great dialectical subtlety in interpretation. His memory, trained on classical texts, was phenomenally active. In one sermon, he could move through the whole Bible, from Paul to Genesis and back again, via the Psalms, piling half-verse on half-verse.

This method of exegesis indeed, which involved creating a whole structure of verbal echoes, linking every part of the Bible, was particularly well-suited to teaching this hitherto quite unknown text, to an audience used to memorizing by ear. And, like a schoolmaster, Augustine tended to present the Bible as a series of cruxes. He never relaxes for a moment the impression of a mind of terrifying acuteness. This hard intellectual quality, tenacious to the point of quibbling, was what

Augustine plainly valued most in himself, and communicated most effectively to his audience. It was the secret of his everyday style—the "subdued" style.

"When it resolves exceptionally difficult problems, comes out with an unexpected demonstration, shows that the speaker can bring out singularly penetrating formulations, as if out of the blue; when it hits on an adversary's weak point, and can expose as fallacious an argument that had seemed unanswerable—all this with a certain stylish touch . . . this can provoke such enthusiastic applause that you would hardly take it for 'subdued.' "

But, above all, there is Augustine's amazing power of integration. He could communicate to perfection the basic idea of the "Word" in the Bible, as an organic whole. His beautiful sermons on the Psalms are quite unique in patristic literature. For, for Augustine, each Psalm had a "single body of feeling that vibrates in every syllable." Each Psalm, therefore, could be presented as a microcosm of the whole Bible—the clear essence of Christianity refracted in the exotic spectrum of a Hebrew poem. Augustine seldom wanders: he "unwinds." A single incident, the juxtaposition of Christ and John the Baptist—is "unraveled" so that the associations of John's statement *"He must grow, and I must diminish"* spread throughout the whole Bible, and come to be reflected even in the rhythm of the seasons.

"There are many things that could be said about S. John the Baptist, but I would never be finished with telling you, nor you with listening. Now let me round it off in a nutshell. Man must be humbled, God must be exalted."

This sense of the particular incident as the vehicle through which an organic whole can find expression accounts for the beauty of Augustine's exegesis. For, as in the incidents of his own life in the *Confessions*, significance suddenly comes to light on a tiny detail. The Father of the Prodigal Son "falls upon his shoulders." It is Christ placing His yoke on the Christian, and in a flash we see the incident as Rembrandt would see it; every line of the heavy figure of the old man charged with meaning. "In some sense or other, Importance is derived from the immanence of infinitude in the finite" [A. Whitehead, *Modes of Thought*].

Augustine preached in this manner for thirty-nine years. The experience influenced him deeply. For Augustine approached his position as a preacher with considerable misgivings. He was a contemplative in the austere tradition of Plotinus. He came near to regarding speech itself as a falling-away of the soul from its inner act of contemplation.

"Nothing can be better, nothing more sweet for me than to gaze upon the Divine treasure without noise and hustle: this is what is sweet and good. To have to preach, to inveigh, to admonish, to edify, to feel responsible for every one of you—this is a great burden, a heavy weight upon me, a hard labor."

As is so often the case with him, Augustine used this tension so creatively just because he could feel so strongly the opposing poles within himself. Thus communication fascinated him.

"For my own way of expressing myself almost always disappoints me. I am anxious for the best possible, as I feel it in me before I start bringing it into the open in plain words; and when I see that it is less impressive than I had felt it to be, I am saddened that my tongue cannot live up to my heart."

The huge pressure built up by the need to communicate will do nothing less than sweep away the elaborate scaffolding of ancient rhetoric. For, as Augustine came to see it at the end of his life, rhetoric had consisted of polishing an end-product, the speech itself, according to elaborate and highly self-conscious rules. It ignored the basic problem of communication: the problems faced by a man burning to get across a message, or by a teacher wanting his class to share his ideas. Immediacy was Augustine's new criterion. Given something worth saying, the way of saying it would follow naturally, an inevitable and unobtrusive accompaniment to the speaker's own intensity; "the thread of our speech comes alive through the very joy we take in what we are speaking about."

The impact, also, was immediate: for the speaker's style was not thought of as a harmonious assemblage of prefabricated parts, which the connoisseur might take to pieces, but rather as the inseparable welding of form and content in the heat of the message, so that "it is a waste of time to tell someone what to admire, if he does not himself sense it." If we read, in the *Confessions*, some passage of full-blooded lyricism and compare it with the stilted language in which the same ideas are expressed in one of Augustine's more "classical" philosophical dialogues, we can immediately see that the Latin language has been fused, has caught alight, in the almost-daily flame of Augustine's sermons.

It is just this intensity which Augustine came to love in the Hebrew prophets. His ear was sensitive to the charm of an exotic language, to a syntax that was after all not so distant from the Punic he could have listened to (and to which he would often refer as some substitute for his ignorance of Hebrew), to the strange appeal of the reiterated phrases of the Psalms, to the names of the towns of Israel that studded a passage "like great lights." But he saw in the prophets, above all, men like himself: men with a message to bring home to a whole "people"—"a hammer shattering the stones."

Augustine lived through the emotions to which he appealed. In his middle age, he became increasingly preoccupied with the idea of a "Mystical Body" of Christ: a body of which Christ was the Head and all true believers the members. For a Platonist, the unity of a body was, above all, a unity of sensations: the soul was the core of the body, for it alone was the center in which all the emotions of the body were experienced. It was this doctrine, which enabled Augustine to put himself in touch with the vast reserves of feeling contained in the Hebrew Scriptures.

For seen in this light, the Psalms were the record of the emotions of Christ and His members. Just as He had taken on human flesh, so Christ had, of his own free will, opened Himself to human feeling. These feelings are only hinted at in the Gospels. Often, the Christ of Augustine's sermons is the pale, impassive figure of a Late Roman mosaic; His Crucifixion is a solemn, measured act of power—"the sleep of a lion." But when he turns to the Psalms, Augustine will draw from them an immensely rich deposit of human emotions: for here was Christ, speaking directly in the person of the passionate King David. The song of the desperate fugitive from the wrath of Saul, is the inner story of the Passion.

"Heaviness fell upon me; and I slept."

"His voice in the Psalms—a voice singing happily, a voice groaning, a voice rejoicing in hope, sighing in its present state—we should know this voice thoroughly, feel it intimately, make it our own."

Augustine's voice, also, will take on richer tones in his later middle age, and especially in the amazing sermons on the "City of God," preached when he was sixty. His sense of the bonds of human feeling will become more acute; and a greater awareness of the pleasures of his audience, of their capacity for love and fear, will seep into his preaching. In these sermons, we begin to hear the songs of Africa. The "sweet melody" of a Psalm sung in the streets, the "serenades," above all, the strange rhythmic chant of the laborers in the fields. It is this chanting in the countryside that will, at last, provide Augustine, the austere Neo-Platonic bishop, with an image worthy of the fullness of the Vision of God.

"So men who sing like this—in the harvest, at the grape-picking, in any task that totally absorbs them—may begin by showing their contentment in songs with words; but they soon become filled with such a happiness that they can no longer express it in words, and, leaving aside syllables, strike up a wordless chant of jubilation."

APPENDIX III

NEVER WITHOUT A
NOTARIUS

ROY J. DEFERRARI

"St. Augustine's Method of Composing and
Delivering Sermons."
American Journal of Philology
Volume 43, 1922. Pages 119–23. *Sine notis.*

Augustine's sermons were recorded and
have been preserved to us through the ecclesiastical shorthand writers. That *notarii* were
present in the church when Augustine
preached is expressly stated by Possidius. He
says, "Even the heretics themselves gathered
together and listened with the Catholics most
eagerly to these books and treatises which is-
sued and flowed forth by the wonderful grace
of God, filled with abundance of reason and
the authority of Holy Scripture; each one
also who would or could, bringing reporters
and taking down what was said." And, "The
Donatists, in particular, who lived in Hippo
and the neighboring towns, brought his addresses and writings to their bishops."

Augustine, too, in a letter to the consuls
Theodosius and Valentinianus, speaks of the

Appendix III

Notarii Ecclesiae. In this letter he quotes from one of his sermons delivered previously, in which he specially called the attention of his audience to the fact that *notarii* were taking down his words and their exclamations of applause.

This common use of the *notarius* in the churches of other early fathers has already been discussed, but in a letter written jointly with Alypius to Aurelius, Bishop of Carthage, Augustine seems to show that it was customary among preachers of the time to leave the shorthand reports of their sermons untranscribed until they saw fit to make use of them. In this letter, Augustine congratulates Aurelius on the excellent sermons which the priests gave in his presence and begs that some of them be sent to him. He says, *"Obsecramus te per eum qui tibi ista donavit, et populum, cui servis, hac per te benedictione perfudit, ut iubeas singulos quos volueris sermones eorum* conscriptos, *et* emendatos *mitti nobis."* The words *conscriptos* and *emendatos* in this connection naturally mean to be written up from the shorthand reports with whatever changes the preacher desired in his more or less extemporaneous and so perhaps careless statements.

Degert makes a great deal of a passage from Possidius to support his belief that Augustine wrote out most of his sermons before delivery. The words of Possidius are, *"Tanta autem ab eodem dictata et edita sunt, tantaque in ecclesia disputata, excepta atque emendata, vel adversus diversos haereticos, vel ex canonicis libris exposita ad aedificationem sanctorum ecclesiae filiorum, ut ea omnia vix quisquam studiosorum perlegere et nosse sufficiat."*

Possidius, however, distinguishes clearly here between Augustine's finished works, dictated *(dictata)* and published *(edita)*, and his disputations in the churches, taken down *(excepta)* and emended *(emendata).* The sense here regarding Augustine's disputations or sermons is clearly the same as that respecting the sermons which Augustine himself speaks of in the passage quoted just above. The discourses were taken down by *notarii*, transcribed from the shorthand notes, and emended before circulation.

Augustine's entire life was very intimately connected with the shorthand writers. That he made use of *notarii* in the privacy of his study, is attested not only by frequent allusions to them, often by name, in his own writings, but also by the statements of Possidius. The latter says, "But when such things had been arranged and set in order, then, as though freed from consuming and annoying cares, his soul rebounded to the more intimate and lofty thoughts of the mind in order either to ponder on the discovery of divine truth or to dictate some of the things already discovered or else to emend some of the works which had been previously dictated and then transcribed."

The intimate and important position of the *notarius* in the life of Augustine and his friends is shown by the manner in which they speak of the shorthand writer in their private correspondence. Thus, to cite only a few out of many passages of this sort, Jerome writes to Augustine and laments the lack, in Palestine, of *notarii* that have a good knowledge of Latin. Evodius writes to Augustine in much distress over the loss of a particularly bright *notarius*. In one instance Augustine has just received a letter from a certain Seleuciana, in which he is informed of the very curious theological opinion of one of his acquaintances. In answering this letter, Augustine, unable to believe that the person in question could have entertained such a belief, suggests that the *notarius* has taken down the letter from dictation inaccurately, or has deliberately falsified the note when copying it into longhand. The possibility of his friend's not having a *notarius* does not enter his mind. Furthermore the discussions of Augustine with his associates at Cassiciacum, taken down by the ever-present *notarius*, form the substance of the books "Against the Academics," "On the Order of Providence," and "On the Happy Life."

Not only did Augustine employ the *notarius* for the well-known duties of the scholar's secretary, but he also found him indispensable for reporting his oral debates with heretics. In such cases the *notarii* acted officially just as court stenographers do today. It was indeed from these shorthand records that Augustine was later able to make the compendium of his various public debates with the Donatists, which now exists under the name, *"Breviculus collationis cum Donatistis."*

Possidius, in recounting the various public debates in which his venerated teacher took part, rarely fails to mention either the *notarius* or his art. Thus a certain *domus regiae procurator* at Carthage discovered a clandestine gathering of Manichaeans, whom he immediately took to a board of bishops and had examined *ad tabulas*. Among these bishops was Augustine himself. Similarly, regarding Augustine's controversies with the Manichaeans Fortunatus (392) and Felix (404), Possidius says, *"Unde condicto die et loco convenerunt in unum, concurrentibus quam plurimis studiosis turbisque curiosis, et apertis notarii tabulis disputatio coepta primo, et secundo finita est die."* And also, *"Cum quodam etiam Felice de numero eorum quos elector dicunt Manichaei, publice in Hipponensi ecclesia notariis excipientibus disputavit populo astante."*

Pascentius, the Arian, once engaged Augustine in a public debate, but contrary to the usual custom, positively forbade the use of the tablets and stylus. Later (427 or 428) Augustine overcame the Arian bishop Maximinus in public debate. From the shorthand accounts of this meeting Augustine was afterwards obliged to publish a recapitulation, since Maximinus had succeeded in spreading incorrect reports about the encounter.

The public debates with the Donatists, however, furnish us with the most interesting incidents regarding this use of *notarii*. The Donatist bishop Emeritus was refuted in public debate, and indeed remained silent so long in the midst of his speech that finally the *notarius* himself urged him to continue. Augustine himself tells us of a striking incident which occurred at his public debate with the Donatist bishop

Fortunatus. The regular *notarii*, for some unknown reason, refused to serve at the contest, regardless of any sort of inducement. Volunteers were summoned from the audience. These, although willing enough, were utterly unable to keep up with the rapid speech of the contestants and were finally obliged to stop writing.

Shorthand experts were employed in behalf of the state as well as the church at the famous conference of Catholic and Donatist bishops at Carthage in 411. Augustine says a great deal in this connection in his public letter summoning all Donatists to the true Church. That part of the letter in which we are interested reads: "Both your bishops and we arrived in Carthage, and, although they were before unwilling and said it was not in accordance with their dignity, we all met. Seven were selected from our number and seven from theirs who were to be representatives in the debate. Then seven more were chosen from each party, with whom the former seven were to take counsel when there was need. Then four were selected from each side to have charge of writing up the proceedings, lest some falsehood be inserted by somebody. Four stenographers also were given by each party to alternate two at a time in doing the work of the judge's stenographers, lest some one of us pretend that something was said which was not taken down. To this great care another caution was added, that both they and we should, just as the judge himself, subscribe to our words, lest some one say afterwards that there had been some meddling, etc., etc."

Thus did Augustine use the *notarius* in his various works, his sermons, letters, debates, and finished productions, and it is hard to believe that the bishop of Hippo himself, one of the busiest of men both in literary and administrative ways, ever performed the mechanical task of mere writing in connection with his literary productions except in the most incidental way. We know that his sermons were taken down by *notarii* as he delivered them. Are we to believe that he performed the mechanical task of copying the shorthand?

BIBLIOGRAPHY

SERMONS IN LATIN

Augustini, S. Aureli Hipponensis Episcopi, *Sermones ad Populum*, Tomus XXXVIII, *Patrologiae Latinae*, apud J.-P. Migne Editorem, Intra Moenia Parisina, MDCCCXLV, Coll. 332–54, 773–75, 997–1039.

SERMONS IN ENGLISH

St. Augustine: Sermons for Christmas and Epiphany. Translated and edited by Thomas Comerford Lawlor. New York: Newman Press, 1952. Volume 15 in the *Ancient Christian Writers Series: The Works of the Fathers in Translation*, edited by Johannes Quasten STD and Joseph C. Plumpe PhD.
Selected Sermons of St. Augustine. Translated and edited by Quincy Howe, Jr. New York: Holt, Rinehart and Winston, 1966.

The *Works of Saint Augustine: A Translation for the 21ˢᵗ Century. Sermons III/Volume 6
(#184–229Z) on the Liturgical Seasons.* Translated by Edmund Hill OP. General
editor of the series, John E. Rotelle OSA. New Rochelle, NY: New City Press,
1993.

RECENT ANTHOLOGIES

Augustine: Major Writings. Compiled and edited by Benedict J. Groeschel, CFR. New
York: Crossroad, 1995. A volume in the *Spiritual Legacy* series.
Augustine of Hippo: Selected Writings. Translation and Introduction by Mary T. Clark.
Preface by Goulven Madec. New York: Paulist Press, 1984. A volume in *The Clas-
sics of Western Spirituality* series.

BIOGRAPHIES

Brown, Peter. *Augustine of Hippo: A Biography.* Berkeley & Los Angeles: University
of California Press, 1967.
Chadwick, Henry. *Augustine.* New York: Oxford University Press, 1996 (1986).
Pope, H. *Saint Augustine of Hippo.* London, 1937; Westminster MD, 1949.
Possidius. *Sancti Augustini Vita.* Edited by Herbert T. Weiskotten. Princeton: Prince-
ton University Press, 1919.
Van der Meer, F. *Augustine the Bishop.* Translated by Brian Battershaw and G. R.
Lamb. New York: Sheed and Ward, 1961.
Wills, Garry. *Saint Augustine: A Penguin Life.* New York: A Lipper/Viking Book,
1999.

BACKGROUND

Aland, Kurt. *A History of Christianity. Volume 1: From the Beginnings to the Threshold
of the Reformation.* Philadelphia: Fortress Press, 1980.
Brown, Peter. *Religion and Society in the Age of St. Augustine.* New York: Harper &
Row, 1972.

Bibliography

Deferrari, Roy J. "St. Augustine's Method of Composing and Delivering Sermons," *American Journal of Philology*, volume 43 (1922), pages 97–123, 193–219.

Frend, W.H.C. *The Rise of Christianity.* Philadelphia: Fortress Press, 1984.

Gilbert, Allan H. "Translation," *Dictionary of World Literature: Criticism, Forms, Technique.* Edited by Joseph T. Shipley. Paterson: Littlefield, Adams & Company, 1960 (1953), page 425.

Grant, Michael. *Ancient History Atlas.* Cartography by Arthur Banks. New York: Macmillan, 1971.

Littell, Franklin H. *The Macmillan Atlas History of Christianity.* Cartography by Emanuel Hausman. Prepared by Carta, Jerusalem. New York: Macmillan Publishing Co., Inc., 1976.

MacMullen, Ramsay. *Christianizing the Roman Empire: A.D. 100–400.* New Haven: Yale University Press, 1984.

McEvedy, Colin. *The Penguin Atlas of Medieval History.* Harmondsworth, UK: Penguin Books, 1961.

Novak, Ralph Martin Jr. *Christianity and the Roman Empire: Background Texts.* Harrisburg: Trinity Press International, 2001.

Pelikan, Jaroslav. *The Excellent Empire: The Fall of Rome and the Triumph of the Church.* San Francisco: Harper & Row, 1988.

Resner, Jr., André. *Preacher and Cross: Person and Message in Theology and Rhetoric.* Grand Rapids: Wm. B. Eerdmans Publishing Company, 1999.

Wilken, Robert L. *The Christians as the Romans Saw Them.* New Haven: Yale University Press, 1984.

ACKNOWLEDGMENTS

Sister Barbara Dupuis, MSC, librarian at Notre Dame Seminary, New Orleans.

The Jesuit priests who taught me Latin over the years: Joseph McCarthy, Paul Ruttle, John Butler, William Scannell, Thomas J. C. Kelly, Martin Ryan, William Carroll, Hayne Martin, Neil Twombley.

Conventiculum apud Universitatem Kentukiae Latinum, regnantibus Terentio Gueneveraque Tunbergiis, quotannis congregandum ad latine solum conversandum quinquaginta hominibus.

ABOUT THE TRANSLATOR

Three encounters with Augustine's Christmas and Epiphany sermons.

I first encountered them sometime in the early 1950s, when I entered the Society of Jesus in New England. There Fr. William Carroll, something of a linguistic and artistic eccentric, introduced us to them around Christmastime. I'd already had five or six years of Latin under my cincture, and was already talking Latin like a magpie—or was it a longshoreman?—around the seminary. Indeed, once I had to talk Latin, all Latin grammar and syntax, which I'd had to master by mindless repetition, seemed to fall into place. Then, I had a manifestation, an epiphany, of my own. Just hearing Augustine's colloquial Latin read aloud by Willy Carroll swept me back to the turn of the fifth century and at the same time carried me up to prose heaven!

The second encounter took place in the early 1960s in New York City. No longer a Jesuit, in the Big Apple to find a job in publishing, I bumped into a bumptious young businesswoman in an evening play-writing class. It was taught by Edward Albee, who was trying to keep himself alive between the one-act *Death of Bessie Smith* and the full-length *Who's Afraid of Virginia Woolf?* Each of the enrolled was promised a dramatic reading of his or her one-act play by professional actors at the Circle in the Square Theatre. Well, she didn't like my play, and I certainly didn't like hers. Few relationships in the history of the world have gotten off to a worse start.

By the second date she revealed that she'd already boarded the Silver Streak, a conversion train heading for God knows where. I smiled and feigned disinterest, able to cope with whatever destination, if not destiny, the Holy Spirit would lead her to. You see, I'd already proposed to her. More to the point, I'd already developed this dangerous habit of proposing on the first date; but she was the first one not to laugh in my face and say no right on the spot.

When Emilie—for that was her name—asked about Mary the mother of Jesus, she wanted to know what the historical hullabaloo was all about. Remembering that Mary had played more than a minor role in Augustine's Christmas sermons, I made a date to meet her at the New York Public Library, Fifth Avenue and Forty-Second Street.

Somehow knowing where Migne's *Patrologia Latina* was to be found, I led her up the main stairs, past the painting of monks (perhaps the first Augustinians) laboring over illuminated manuscripts with a war raging outside the window of their copy room, through the forest of mahogany card catalogs, on into the main reading room, up a winding metal staircase to the balcony.

I plucked the right volume, found the right page, and handed it over to her, saying something like "If you don't read Latin, I'll be glad to help." Looking up, she replied, with what I thought was just a little too much Tabasco (she was from New Orleans), "But I do read Latin!"

There, in the sermons delivered probably in the last quarter of the fourth century and the first quarter of the fifth century, she found popular and patristic enthusiasm for Mary in full bloom, and I found a wife for life.

The third encounter took place when Doubleday editor Trace Murphy asked me, supposedly a seasoned veteran in American religious publishing, what I thought might be missing from the Image Books line. Augustine's Christmas Sermons was my first thought. They already had a *Confessions* and a *City of God*. These and indeed some other titles in their backlist appeared to be aging Cadillacs; that's to say, they had a gleaming past, but it was getting harder to keep the gloss high. A bright new *Sermons* might just add some flash to the parking lot.

As for my Latin, over the years, I've edited a four-book Latin series for high schools. I've written *epistolae* to famous ecclesiastics trying to sign up a book or two as an acquiring editor at Macmillan. I've read Cicero and Augustine aloud with my wife and her recently blinded college professor friend. I've spoken Latin at the *Conventiculum Latinum*, the annual omnium-gatherum at the University of Kentucky of academics and other misfits, unionists all for a better Latin around the world. I've even translated Beatrix Potter's *The Adventures of Peter Rabbit* into Latin ("Too bad it's already been done!") and Thomas à Kempis's *De Imitatione Christi* into English ("An astonishingly fresh translation of the great spiritual classic!").

—WILLIAM GRIFFIN
*Kalendis Januariis MMII*⁰

Printed in the United States
by Baker & Taylor Publisher Services